MW01634826

AN IMPOSSIBLE DREAM IS MADE POSSIBLE by passion. If you have a dream or goal that has always been on your mind, this book from John Brink will help you go after it!

—JIM GOOD, FOUNDER OF GOODSIR NATURE PARK

FINDING YOUR PASSION

LIVING THE DREAM

WRITING ASSISTANCE Guy Saddy

ART DIRECTOR Grace LaFrance

COPY EDITOR Pamela Swanigan

PROOFREADER Pamela Swanigan

Published by Brink Media. Prince George, British Columbia.

Page 179, photo courtesy of BergMedia Creative Agency; back cover flap
and pages 87, 89, 96, 99 and 100, photos courtesy of Kay Collective; pages
88, 97, photos courtesy of BB Photography; page 92 photo courtesy of
Sharon Brink; page 1 photo courtesy of Derek Flynn Media; photo page
2 courtesy of Focal Point Studios; photo page 3 courtesy of Tara's Tilted
Tripod; page 5 photo courtesy of Alex Mackenzie.

Library and Archives Canada Cataloguing in Publication
Brink, John A., 1940– author
        Finding Your Passion, Living the Dream / John A. Brink

ISBN 978-1-7781546-1-4

Printed and bound in Canada by Friesens Corporation.

This book is dedicated to my wife, Sharon, and my daughters,
Nicole and Tina, as well as those who understand the true
power of passion and possess the audacity to chase their dreams
with unwavering determination.

FOREWORD

ASK A WISE PERSON what they most desire in this world, and they will most likely say, "Give me more wisdom."

It gives me great pleasure to introduce John Brink's third book, *Finding Your Passion, Living the Dream*. As a fellow author and motivational speaker, I have had the privilege of witnessing firsthand the power of John's message and his ability to inspire people to pursue their dreams.

The John Brink I know lives his life dream with purpose, passion, dedication, and sheer hard work. John writes from personal experience. He started pursuing his passions during his first few days in Canada and hasn't slowed down since, staying determined and inspired to succeed.

In his powerful, thought-provoking third book, John demonstrates that anything worth having is never given to you on a silver platter. It takes imagination, hard work, going the extra mile, focus, determination, and never giving up.

In this book, John shares his personal journey of discovering his passion and offers practical advice on how to identify and pursue your own passions. He reminds us that passion is the fuel that drives us towards our goals, and that living a life without passion is like driving a car with an empty tank.

In 2019, the Province of British Columbia presented John with the Order of British Columbia for his many years of service to this province. I have had the pleasure of knowing John for many years and can attest to his authenticity and commitment to helping others achieve their full potential. His passion for life is infectious, and his message is one that resonates with people of all ages and backgrounds.

If you want to be inspired to be more than you are today, his third book will show you the way. John reminds us that success is not measured by material possessions, but by the impact we make on the world and the joy we feel in our hearts. Read this book, learn from John, apply his wisdom, and activate these lessons in your own life.

—DR. PETER LEGGE, OBC, LL.D (HON.), DTECH

THE PASSION PRINCIPLE

I'M SITTING AT THE DESK in my library. This room is my sanctuary and holds much meaning for me. The books that line my shelves are a comfort, but so is this place that I am fortunate enough to call home. I live in North Saanich, a Vancouver Island bedroom community close to Victoria, British Columbia. The setting here is stunning. Seventy-foot-tall fir trees sway in a gentle breeze, and a light rain envelops our beautiful house in mist. It is a sanctuary within a sanctuary within a sanctuary.

Considering my back story, the fact that I'm here in this place, surrounded by books and calm and nature, is no small thing. My journey to where I am today has been long and challenging. Almost six decades have passed since 1965, when I left my home in Holland to come to Canada. By the time I reached Prince George, the largest city in central British Columbia, I had $25.47 in the pocket of my pants. I carried one bag, which contained a change of clothes and three heavy books: *Management*, by Peter R. Drucker; *Logical Thinking*, by A.B. Roels; and *Encyclopedia of Canadian History*, a way for me to understand and appreciate my new home. Today, they double as markers of my journey's beginnings and are stacked atop one another in my library.

When I first arrived in B.C., the odds against me achieving success were far higher than the odds for it. To an outside observer, what seemed to lie in store for me didn't look too secure. I was 24 years old and spoke no English. I also had very little formal education, as I'd left school after failing Grade 7 three times in a row. My dismal scholastic record was, I learned much later in life, directly related to a significant developmental disability: like so many children, I had been shaped by attention-deficit/hyperactivity disorder, or ADHD. (This condition continues to define me today—mostly for good.)

In addition to my belongings, all I'd brought with me to begin my life in Canada was a steely determination to have my own lumber mill. It was my dream, fed and nurtured for the previous two decades of my life. But unlike so many dreamers, I firmly believed that this was my destiny and that it was within reach. Nothing could divert me from the path ahead.

The reason was simple. I chased that dream with tenacity, with determination—and, ultimately, with *passion*.

———

From meagre beginnings, I scraped and fought my way to incredible heights. After starting as a clean-up man at a local mill, I eventually reached my goal of owning a lumber mill—and much, much more. For a time, I did my best Sisyphus impression: after achieving what many would call "success," I almost lost it all and came close to declaring bankruptcy—twice. But armed with a single-minded commitment to claw back what I'd lost and soar above my previous successes, I returned stronger and with more to show for my efforts than I'd had before.

Today, under the auspices of The Brink Group, I own more than a dozen companies. They encompass several different industries, from real-estate development and logistics to sawmilling and the creation and sale of secondary manufactured-lumber products. This last business is the one that first defined my life as an entrepreneur. Using proprietary technology that we developed here in Prince George, we take small, less-desirable pieces of wood and join them together to create wooden studs that are stronger and less prone to warping than our competitors' products. This a big deal in hot and humid climates, such as parts of the southern United States, and it was the innovation that founded my business career.

But there is more to me than the businesses I've built. I'm a pilot, currently on the hunt for my commercial aviator's licence. I do competitive bodybuilding, a sport I took up at the rather ripe age of 76. Shortly after starting, I entered my first competition, the Vancouver Pro/Am. I ended up qualifying for both the Nationals and the Arnolds, the most prestigious tournament in the world. Today, at 82, I'm the oldest competitive bodybuilder in North America.

In between my businesses, flying planes, and bodybuilding, I've found time for a few other pursuits. I'm an in-demand public speaker—not bad for someone who used to freeze when asked to talk in front of anything but the mirror! I'm a podcaster (check out *On the Brink* wherever you get your podcasts) and a dedicated dressage rider, a hobby I share with my wife, Sharon. On many occasions I've advised the British Columbia government on forestry-related concerns, and my input is sought by the highest provincial officials when major industry decisions are made. In 2019, in recognition of my philanthropic and community service, I was awarded the Order of British Columbia, the province's highest honour.

I'm also a published author. My memoir, *Against All Odds: How Attitude, Passion, and Work Ethic Lead to Success*, was released to enthusiastic acclaim in 2021. And my second effort, *ADHD Unlocked*, a book that helps reveal the incredible positives for those of us who are "blessed" with ADHD, was published in 2022. Not too bad for a non-native English speaker who failed Grade 3…and Grade 7 three times!

How do I do it?

The answer is contained in the subtitle to my original memoir: *attitude, passion, and work ethic*. It is my credo, if you will. Each of these elements is extremely important to the pursuit of success. I think of them as a three-legged stool: when you take away one leg, the whole thing collapses.

That said, there is a hierarchy. While both work ethic and attitude are important, they stem from passion. Without passion as the motivational driver, the other two elements will be impossible to sustain—or, in the greater scheme of things, simply rendered meaningless.

Passion is the jet fuel that propels us forward toward greater and greater things. And it is passion that can lift us up when we fail or when we face challenges that seem endlessly daunting. When it comes down to it, passion is the factor that can push a person on toward a meaningful and accomplished life.

———

As with my previous book, *ADHD Unlocked*, *Finding Your Passion, Living the Dream* uses a question-and-answer format. Partly this reflects my own desire to serve up my experiences—and the experiences of the other remarkable people who have generously contributed their stories—in a way that is easily digestible. You can bounce around from chapter to chapter; I know that's what I do. (Perfect for the ADHD in me!) But the other reason that I've opted to indulge my inner Socrates is that the quickest and most effective route to knowledge is to relentlessly question. To challenge others, of course. But most importantly, to challenge ourselves.

In diving into the topic of passion, I found I was also embarking upon a voyage into the depths of my self. For those of us who have tapped into it, passion is woven into who we are on an elemental level. To understand your passion—to fully grasp what excites you and drives you on—is to thoroughly understand who you are at your core. It's a path that cuts to your essence, a gateway to the soul.

This is not a self-help book—although, depending on how you use its message, it certainly could be. And it isn't just a litany of inspirational tales, although it features many. Instead, think of it as an exploration of what passion is and what it means to us. It examines how we can create the conditions for passion to emerge, and how passion, once acquired, can push us on to create our best lives.

Passion is a nuanced concept. The way it expresses itself can vary across individuals and, indeed, even time and space—depending on where in the world you are located or which century you happen to be born into. And there are downsides to passion, which we will not ignore: just because something inflames your interest does not always mean that it's all positive. For example, as someone who was born into a war that claimed more lives than any other, I'm acutely aware that many Nazis were very passionate about their vision for a reordered world. So we're left with the possibility, which we'll explore, that passion can be destructive—or obstructive, if it exists discordantly within a person.

It is also true that living a passionate life is not the same as living an easy life. Ultimately, though, it is the way forward to your own adventure, one that is waiting to be written. And that's a much more meaningful goal than any conventional measure of "success." Finding passion—and acting from a passionate place—will pave the way for a fulfilling life. This I guarantee.

> **Do not fear failure but rather fear not trying.**
>
> —ROY T. BENNETT, AUTHOR

In pursuing your passion, at some points you will undoubtedly stumble. That's okay, and that's what goals are for. As author Roy T. Bennett once wrote, "Do not fear failure but rather fear not trying." This is the only route forward for those who are committed to "living the dream."

With warmest regards,

JOHN A. BRINK

THE HEART OF PASSION

—

Although the word "passion" may seem straightforward, a discussion of what it actually means turns out to be more complex than one might think. Does it vary according to time, place, and circumstances? Does culture play a role in shaping how passion is expressed? Is passion always positive, or can some types be damaging? Are some people inherently passionate? Can we even attempt a one-size-fits-all definition?

OKAY, LET'S CUT TO THE CHASE: HOW DO YOU DEFINE PASSION?

You're starting off with the big one, hey? Okay, let's try and nail it down. But first I need to say that looking at "passion" is like looking at a multifaceted diamond. What we see shifts depending on perspective. And that angle can be affected by many factors.

LIKE WHAT?

Like which point we're at in the history of humankind, for example. Or where you are in your own timeline. There are many variables. But let me start by trying to define what passion means to *me*.

First, it must be something that resonates on an almost primary level. In other words, it should excite, satisfy, challenge, or touch something deep within you. Second, it should be something that is important in your life: passions need to *matter*. And finally, it should be something that lasts. Passions endure over time. Think of an epic love affair, not a one-night stand or a pleasant flirtation, so to speak.

IT'S INTERESTING THAT YOU WENT STRAIGHT TO PASSIONATE LOVE TO ILLUSTRATE YOUR POINT.

I went there for one simple reason: romantic love is so distinct from the type of passion I'm about to talk about that it qualifies as a difference in kind. Really, within the context of this book, it's more like a distant cousin of the passion we're going to explore than a close relative.

Sure, people are passionate about other people. We've been force-fed the perfection of passionate romantic love since time immemorial. We all know the story of Romeo and Juliet, but have you ever thought about how limited in scope their passion was? This wasn't some epic romance that ran over the course of decades. These were two children who were infatuated with each other. Honestly, in terms of real passion—the kind that endures and perhaps grows over years—it doesn't even pass the smell test. Exciting? Yes. Hormonal? You bet. But enduring? Not even close.

OKAY, I GET YOUR POINT. SO ACCORDING TO YOUR DEFINITION, WOULD MY PASSION FOR ICE CREAM QUALIFY?

Ha! Interesting. You may like ice cream. You may even *love* ice cream. Perhaps you have loved it ever since you were a child. But in the grand arc of your life, does ice cream really *matter*? Does it truly engage you? Does it resonate some place deep within the very core of your being? I'm going out on a limb here, but I don't think so. (Unless, of course, your passion is *making* ice cream and you spend your days coming up with innovative new combinations of ingredients. That's a whole different discussion!)

Here's another bit of texture. What kind of hardship would you be willing to endure in order to have ice cream? If you were denied it, to what lengths would you go to ensure a supply? Are you prepared to suffer to have it?

YOU'RE BEING RIDICULOUS NOW.

Not entirely. Because real passion also demands dedication, perseverance and, occasionally, sacrifice. If you are truly passionate about something, these are the kind of lengths you'll go to in order to pursue it.

WELL, I WON'T BE DOING ANY OF THAT FOR A BOWL OF ICE CREAM.

Exactly. But people who go after their passion—the kind of person who will dedicate themselves to the pursuit of something that excites them at their core—are willing to give up things of significance to do it. They don't always have to. But they are willing to.

This may be the reason that the original meaning of "passion" was "to suffer."

SERIOUSLY? "TO SUFFER"? HOW DOES THAT MAKE SENSE?

"Passion" comes from the Latin word *patior* (or *passio*), which literally means to suffer or endure. You can find similar meanings in English today. For example, "compassion"—a feeling of sympathy for someone who is going through something difficult—adds the prefix "com" to the root "passion" to form the meaning "suffer together." Even the term "passive" has "passion" at its root, though you may not make the connection automatically. A dictionary definition of Middle English terms would likely categorize passivity as a state of "being capable of being acted upon." In other words, the passive person is the hapless recipient of a negative experience or act. In their passivity, they are primed to *suffer*.

Passion in the sense of "suffering" also figures prominently in Christian imagery. You know Christ's final walk down the Via Dolorosa (the "Way of Suffering") through ancient Jerusalem—wearing a crown of thorns mockingly presented by Pontius Pilate and carrying on his back the cross upon which he'd be executed? That's known as "The Passion."

HONESTLY, I'D NEVER MADE THE CONNECTION. BUT REALLY, ISN'T THIS ANCIENT HISTORY? IS "SUFFERING" STILL A CORE INGREDIENT OF PASSION?

Not necessarily. But those who are passionately committed to something—it could be an idea, an art, a way of life, a business, social justice—are often willing to experience a level of pain, hardship, or discomfort if that's what it takes. In recent times, we've seen this kind of "passionate suffering" take place on a global scale. From the anti-government protestors in Iran to the Ukrainian resistance fighters who made life difficult for Vladimir Putin, no one would say that these people didn't suffer in service of their passion—which in both cases is to simply be free.

These are just two examples. There are many injustices in the world. And there are many brave people willing to sacrifice all they have in service of their passion for the greater good.

BUT THESE ARE EXCEPTIONAL SITUATIONS. DID YOU EVER SUFFER FOR YOUR PASSION?

Let me tell you a bit about my first year in Canada, and you can decide.

I flew out of Amsterdam and landed in Montreal in the summer of 1965. At the age of 24, with $150 in my pocket and no command of English whatsoever, I was headed to the forests of British Columbia, the best place on earth to pursue my passion.

What passion, you ask? Ever since I was a young boy, I'd had a dream: to head up my own lumber mill. At this point, it was something I'd been working toward my entire life. When I was forced to quit school after failing Grade 7 three times, I went to work at a furniture-manufacturing facility, a job my father—who was in management at a local lumber mill—arranged for me. By my early 20s, I was working at the same facility as my dad, eventually as part of a roving team of auditors. It was a very prestigious position, one that came with significant responsibility. I was the youngest member on the audit team, and that was a bit of a feather in my cap.

But working for a company owned by other people, especially in relatively conservative Holland, would never allow me to do what I needed to do. And in terms of corporate advancement, I knew my lack of educational qualifications would always get in my way. So I didn't just "decide" to emigrate. From my perspective, I *needed* to.

> **When you're following your energy and doing what you want all the time, the distinction between work and play dissolves.**
>
> —SHAKTI GAWAIN, AUTHOR

WHAT HAPPENED AFTER YOU ARRIVED?

From Montreal, I took a train to Vancouver, where I kicked around for a couple of days, burning through much of the rest of my nest egg, such as it was. As luck would have it, though, at the Granville Street office of Immigration Canada, I was served by a German-speaking officer. Like most Dutch citizens, I had some knowledge of German. After I had explained my background and my dream of owning a sawmill, he said to me, "You should go to Prince George. There are lots of jobs for someone like you, and the forest industry is booming." That was all I needed to hear. After a 20-hour bus ride, I finally arrived in Prince George, B.C.

With me, I had one suitcase with a change of clothes and three books, none of which I'd actually read all the way through.

WHAT AN ODD DETAIL! WHY HADN'T YOU READ THE BOOKS?

I simply couldn't get through one from cover to cover. As you'll recall, I performed miserably in school. It was only several decades later that I learned what lay behind my difficulties: attention-deficit/hyperactivity disorder, or ADHD. This shaped me in profound ways. Much of who I am, including what motivates me, is directly related to it. We'll see how, and to what extent, a little later in this book.

But back to the story. After I arrived, I got a job almost immediately. But it wasn't in Prince George: it was at a mill in Quesnel, about an hour-and-a-half drive south. It went well, for a time. However, after I refused to join the union, I was forced to look for another job. I found one, or so I thought, back in Prince George, at the Netherlands Overseas Mill.

I was excited to be going back to Prince George, a larger city that offered more opportunity. Before I arrived, I was promised a position based on my qualifications. But when I showed up, day after day after day…there was never any work.

Every morning, I would walk the eight kilometres from Prince George to the mill where my job was "waiting." And every day, I had to turn around and walk back. There was one more component to this dismal ritual: after walking back to town, I'd drop in at the post office, hoping to collect the money owed me from my previous position. And every day, I would leave empty-handed. My final paycheque from my job in Quesnel never arrived.

Finally, with no money for food or shelter, I ended up sleeping in an old unused cabin on the Netherlands Overseas Mill property. I figured they owed me that much, at least. But it was now September, and the freezing Canadian winter was closing in. The cabin was unheated. There was no power. At some point, I realized that I hadn't eaten for 10 days.

WHAT DID YOU DO THEN?

I was really out of options. I began to worry that I'd die in the cold

> **You don't choose your passions: your passions choose you.**
>
> —JEFF BEZOS, AMAZON CEO

and dark if I stayed in the cabin. So I walked back to Prince George and began sleeping under a tree outside the hospital. That way, if things really went south I'd at least have a chance of being saved.

Finally I'd had enough. I decided to hitchhike back to Quesnel to try and find out what had happened to my paycheque. After arriving in town, I went to my former boarding house and knocked on the door. Mrs. McEwen, the boarding-house owner, opened it.

"Oh my God!" she said, and she ushered me inside.

She was shocked at my appearance. My clothes were rough and dirty. I had lost at least 15 pounds and was probably malnourished by this point. This was my introduction to my new life in central British Columbia. But even in those dark, uncertain times, I never gave up on my desire to own my lumber mill—a goal that I'd eventually achieve.

Now, that's passion.

I CERTAINLY CAN'T ARGUE WITH THAT. BUT SURELY YOU'RE NOT SAYING THAT THE ONLY WAY TO PURSUE PASSION IS THROUGH THIS KIND OF TRIAL BY FIRE, ARE YOU?

No, not at all. I'm telling you this story to illustrate that when you truly have a passionate commitment, you're prepared to do what it takes to see it through. That's not to say that there isn't a spectrum of passion: I believe there is.

CAN YOU ELABORATE? WHAT WOULD A "SPECTRUM OF PASSION" LOOK LIKE?

At one end there lives a quiet, almost low-key commitment to whatever it is you're passionate about. Toward this edge, you'll find people who are invested in an activity—let's use quilting, for example—and who have stuck with this activity for years. They get a lot out of it, of course. Otherwise, why do it for any significant length of time? But often, this kind of low-level attachment more adequately describes an "enjoyable activity" than a full-on passion.

YOU MEAN LIKE A HOBBY?

Well, yes and no. (I told you this might get complicated!) Listen, I definitely believe that hobbies can also be passions, and passions that are kept on the periphery of a person's life are often called hobbies. Say a person plays piano. Maybe she even dabbled at playing piano for a living, at some point. She's good at it, maybe even very good. And by playing almost every day, she's consistently getting better—honing her chops, as a musician might put it. There's no question that the act of playing the piano—of *being a pianist*—is a defining part of who she is. It might even be *the* defining part: when her epitaph is being carved in granite for all eternity, it might read, "Above all else, she was an excellent pianist."

Why was it not the central feature of her life? Why had she decided not to make it her career? Perhaps she couldn't fit it into the way her world was structured. Maybe she was a single mother who had to prioritize getting food on the table over pursuing her art. Perhaps she hated the hours or hanging around in bars. But that certainly doesn't diminish the passion that drove her to become a fantastic musician. So even though she didn't—or perhaps thought she

> **Passion rebuilds the world for the youth. It makes all things alive and significant.**
>
> —RALPH WALDO EMERSON, POET

couldn't—make the kind of choices that allowed her to make a living at what she loved, she was nevertheless passionate about playing piano.

But we'll talk more about this distinction a little later on.

SO WHAT'S THE DISTINCTION BETWEEN A "LOW-KEY" PASSION AND ONE THAT LIVES ON THE OTHER END OF THE SPECTRUM?

Well, the impact on your life if you were forced to abandon the pursuit entirely, for one. Here's an example. Say you're a chef at a Michelin-starred restaurant. Your passion, obviously, is creating exceptional dishes. Let's say that after coming down with COVID-19, you discover that your senses of taste and smell are gone; as you know, this is a common side effect for some people. You can't cook because you can't taste. Now let's say that this condition turns out to be permanent.

> **Life is like riding a bicycle. To keep your balance, you must keep moving.**
>
> —ALBERT EINSTEIN, PHYSICIST

Can you imagine how that would make you feel? You'd be devastated, at the very least. Your entire world would be turned upside down.

Now on the other hand, there are some pursuits that are enjoyable commitments, but not too much more. Maybe you're a big fan of Wordle, the *New York Times* word-finding puzzle. You play it daily. You're somewhat addicted to it, even. But is it a defining part of your life? Would you suffer for Wordle? Would your world be turned upside down if you couldn't play it? If so, I'm a little worried!

OKAY, I CAN SEE IT'S A MATTER OF DEGREES.

Exactly!

SO IF SOMETHING QUALIFIES AS A PASSION, IT'S ALL GOOD, THEN?

No—in fact, not at all. But before we explore this further, I'd like to talk about the two different ways that passion is expressed. On one hand there is harmonious passion—on the other, obsessive passion.

CAN YOU EXPLAIN THIS A BIT MORE?

I'll do my best, but first let's give credit where credit is due. The concepts and this distinction aren't mine. They come from University of Quebec at Montreal (UQAM) psychologist Robert J. Vallerand, whose 2015 book, *The Psychology of Passion*, is the definitive word on the subject. Vallerand is one of the foremost researchers on the psychology of passion and one of the very few who has dedicated much of his career to the subject.

IT SEEMS ODD THAT THERE AREN'T MORE PEOPLE STUDYING PASSION. IT SEEMS LIKE IT'S ON EVERYONE'S MIND LATELY.

It's quite astonishing, really. If you do a Google search for "passion," you'll get 2.62 *billion* results! Yet for a concept that is so critical, so discussed, and so often cited, there are surprisingly few academic studies that have tried to draw a bead on what passion is and how it works within our lives.

SO WHAT DID VALLERAND COME UP WITH? WHAT DID HE CONCLUDE?

His main contribution to has been to propose what he calls "The Dualistic Model of Passion," or DMP. Here's a summary of Vallerand's theory:

> *The DMP defines passion as a strong inclination toward a self-defining activity that one likes (or even loves), finds important (or highly values), and in which one invests time and energy. It is proposed that there are two types of passion, obsessive and harmonious, that can be distinguished in terms of how the passionate activity has been internalized into one's identity.*
>
> *Obsessive passion results from a controlled internalization of the activity into one's identity. A controlled internalization originates from intra and/or interpersonal pressure typically because certain contingencies are attached to the activity. Conversely, harmonious passion results from an autonomous internalization of the activity into the person's identity. An autonomous internalization occurs when individuals have freely accepted the activity as important for them without any contingencies attached to it. Harmonious passion is hypothesized to lead to positive outcomes while obsessive passion leads to less adaptive outcomes.[1]*

While the definition is academically dry, it is also very specific.

UH, SURE...BUT CAN YOU TRANSLATE IT INTO ENGLISH?

Although I'm reluctant to put words into Vallerand's mouth, in a nutshell I think he means that obsessive passions are ones that people pursue not just for the thing in itself, but also

> **Finding meaning in your life is not a difficult thing, but it is harder than living a numb, fast-paced superficial life.**
>
> —JUANITA GOMEZ, WRITER

[1]From https://www.lrcs.uqam.ca/en/results/dualistic-model-of-passion-dmp/

for other outcomes and benefits that the thing may bring them. "If I become great at X, a positive byproduct will be Y." X could be, to use our previous example, playing piano at a world-class level. Y could be feelings of pride and self-worth, or fame, or money. In other words, these outcomes rely on pursuing the passion; they are contingent on them.

By contrast, harmonious passions don't come loaded with those contingencies. The activity delights or challenges or captivates us on its own, for reasons that have little to do with approval, recognition, and so on. The passion is central to our identity, but in a way that isn't linked with any external pressures or caveats. In a way, harmonious passion meshes with who we are and what our lives are like. It doesn't come freighted with, say, the baggage of other people's expectations or, probably worse, negative self-judgement.

But there's more to obsessive passion than this. Sometimes, an obsessive passion can compel someone to do things that perhaps aren't in their best interests.

HOW SO?

I'll take it from the horse's mouth. In a 2007 paper titled "On the Psychology of Passion: In Search of What Makes People's Lives Most Worth Living," Vallerand uses the example of a university professor who also happens to be obsessed with playing guitar, to the point where he simply can't stop himself from jamming—even though he has to prepare a presentation for the following day. Vallerand writes, "He might have difficulties focusing on the task at hand (playing music) and may not experience as much positive affect and flow as he should while playing."

Well, sure. Not to mention the fact that he has likely sabotaged his professional career by not fully preparing for his important talk. But the takeaway in the above situation is that obsessive passion can exert control over the person instead of the other way around.

OKAY, THAT MAKES SENSE.

Before we go any further, however, I'd like to take a closer look at how Vallerand defines passion, at least in terms of the DMP: "*a strong inclination toward a self-defining activity that one likes (or even loves), finds important (or highly values), and in which one invests time and energy.*" I think this pretty much aligns with our more everyday definition.

To boil it down to the essentials, passion is predicated on something being so important to you that you spend a lot of time doing it—and that, in the end, it's so integral to who you are that it helps define you. *I am a pianist. I am a software developer. I am a freedom fighter for my people.*

In my books, that's a very powerful combination.

IS OBSESSIVE PASSION ALWAYS HARMFUL?

That's a really good question. I strongly believe the answer is "No." But there are caveats. First, studies suggest that harmonious passions are more likely to lead to "more adaptive outcomes," as Vallerand states—for our purposes, that means outcomes that are deemed "healthy," or something positive in our lives. Obsessive passions are less likely to lead us down the same path. With the latter, self-esteem often depends on the outcome of the pursuit. Plus, as we've seen, the desire to engage with one's passion can be almost

> **We don't have bosses cracking a whip. How do you execute this stuff if you're not a little obsessed?**
>
> —MICHAEL MABBOTT, FILMMAKER

out of control—an urge that cannot be resisted. This can open the door to behaviours that can be less than desirable. Vallerand calls these "maladaptive," but "unhealthy," in my opinion, would be the best way to put it, at least for our non-academic purposes.

To sum up: adaptive, or healthy, outcomes are often linked with harmonious passion, while maladaptive, or unhealthy, outcomes are more closely associated with obsessive passion.

OKAY, I THINK I HEAR YOU.

However, to further confuse things, just because your passion is obsessive doesn't necessarily mean that it's *entirely* negative. For example, take your average—or way-above-average—NFL quarterback. Let's call him "Tom Brady." I don't think that I'm going out on a limb here in saying that, within the scheme of Brady's life, football has pretty much been top of mind. If he's having a hard time falling asleep, I'd wager he probably runs plays in his head instead of, say, counting sheep. With good reason, he is widely considered the greatest football player of all time, the G.O.A.T

> **My partner might not agree with this, but I think there are productive things in the obsessiveness.**
>
> —MICHAEL MABBOTT

As of this writing, the guy has just retired at the age of 45. That's positively ancient in NFL quarterback years: there is no way that he should have been taking snaps, let alone getting sacked by 300-pound defensive linemen whose mission in life was to put him out of the game. Yet until recently, he did it, every Sunday, week after week after week. That he came back after "retiring" once before speaks volumes about what kind of guy he is.

And it also says a lot about the kind of passion that lives within him. I'd place good money on Brady's passion being solidly in the obsessive camp. He may love the game. He may also love his ex-wife, Gisele Bündchen. But in pursuing his desire to play football, to this outside observer it's pretty clear that he has sacrificed much in order to keep the game in his life, possibly against his better judgement. The timing of the Brady–Bündchen split, so close to Brady's return to football, does not seem coincidental.

> **Passion will always move you in the direction of your authentic self.**
>
> —DANIELLE LAPORTE, WRITER AND SPEAKER

But if winning football games is Brady's true passion, then maybe he's doing exactly what he wants to do, regardless of the impact on his life. (And the lives of those closest to him. Let's not forget that his decisions will also impact his wife and family, likely in profound ways.) If that's truly the case, can we call his obsession with winning "maladaptive" or "unhealthy"?

Of course, there's a certain amount of judgement involved here, but if we're talking about *Brady himself*, I don't think we can use those terms. Like others before him, Brady is willing to sacrifice—to suffer—for his passion. And, as noted, perhaps sacrifice his family for it. There are costs associated with pursuing this end goal, especially at Brady's level. Maybe he's willing to pay the price.

I DON'T KNOW…THAT DOESN'T SEEM PARTICULARLY HEALTHY TO ME.

I understand. The problem with defining things like "healthy/ unhealthy" and "adaptive/maladaptive" is that they're subjective, or even loaded, terms. And I think this is where some of the difficulty lies. My takeaway: what may be unhealthy for one person may be fine or acceptable for someone else. Even Vallerand makes room for the possibility that obsessive passion is not always a negative thing:

> *We would not want to portray obsessive passion as being completely negative. While it may not lead to outcomes as adaptive as those derived from harmonious passion, obsessive passion is still more adaptive than being nonmotivated or amotivated. Indeed, among other things, it promotes long-term commitment and persistence in the passionate activity.*

There is likely a spectrum where dysfunction intersects passion. At one end, there are people who are totally obsessed with an activity, and it controls their lives. Their identity is so wrapped up in their passion that it crosses a line. But where does that line exist? Even if your passion is supposedly harmonious, I believe there can be obsessive elements to it.

This almost always holds true for those involved in the arts: painters, writers, actors, sculptors. To produce work for, generally speaking, so little financial reward, the act of "suffering" is almost baked into the artists' way. As Michael Mabbott, director of the award-winning mockumentary *The Life and Hard Times of Guy Terrifico*, told me, "We don't have bosses cracking a whip. How do you execute this stuff if you're not a little obsessed?"

MICHAEL MABBOTT: The Storyteller

BORN: December 12, 1972

PASSION: Telling tall tales

CLAIM TO FAME: Directed and wrote his first award-winning feature film, starring music superstars Kris Kristofferson, Merle Haggard, Ronnie Hawkins, Jim Cuddy, and Levon Helm—while flat broke and living in East Vancouver, B.C.

WORDS OF WISDOM: "If you're passionate, then you need to sit down at your fucking desk and type."

But it's also the *rigidity* of the obsessively passionate that differentiates them. "Oftentimes," Vallerand writes, "they can't help but to engage in the passionate activity because ego-invested rather than integrative self-processes are at play." Eventually, those who are obsessively passionate will come to be "dependent on the activity"—addicted to their passion, in other words, sometimes in the same way that an alcoholic craves booze. Plus, their sense of self-worth is often inextricably attached to their passion. So they are compelled to pursue their passion in order to feel good about themselves.

This is very different from harmonious passion, where the activity that you love is integrated into your life and personality in a less consuming and perhaps "healthier" way.

But back to our obsession with the obsessive. The lack of control over passion—one of the hallmarks of the obsessively passionate—is one reason that "passion" as a concept has historically had a rough ride.

WHAT DO YOU MEAN? HOW HAS PASSION HAD A "ROUGH RIDE"?

It has to do with the implications of passion as it relates to control. There are a lot of historical references to passion trumping logic or reason or rational thought—as if it were a volatile emotion which, once unleashed, will inevitably run amok. As a result, in previous centuries especially, passion was often viewed as the antithesis of rational thought.

For example, Cicero, the statesman and writer of ancient Rome, had this to say about the relationship between passion and reason: "He only employs his passion who can make no use of his reason." Even U.S. Founding Father Benjamin Franklin—along with Thomas Jefferson one of America's most prominent Renaissance men—advised caution when indulging passion: "If passion drives you, let reason hold the reins." And returning to *Romeo and Juliet* for a moment, you don't even have to look at the lead characters for a cynical take on obsessive passion: it is the passionate family feud between the Montagues and the Capulets that sets the stage for the ultimate tragedy.

> "I picked up garbage when I was in Grade Four and stuff. I've always had the activist spirit. I guess the age of 16 would be [when I made] my first foray into activism.
>
> —EMILY KELSALL

There are many quotes and tales like these. Taken together, they're variations on a similar theme: that passion is uncontrollable, unpredictable, unsteadying—and, overall, unhelpful or even dangerous. To be avoided at any cost!

BUT SURELY THIS HAS CHANGED DRAMATICALLY IN THE LAST CENTURY OR SO? IT HARDLY SEEMS TO BE THE CASE NOW.

It has changed, certainly. But we only have to look to former Canadian Prime Minister Pierre Trudeau to see the attitude reflected in a more contemporary setting. Trudeau's credo was "La raison avant la passion." In English it means "reason before passion" or, more commonly, "reason over passion." Trudeau himself was often accused of displaying an almost Spock-like intellectual coldness, especially when dealing with certain parts of Canada where Liberal Party prospects weren't all that great.

That said, his commitment to replacing the British North America Act with a made-in-Canada Constitution, and his defense of a unified Canada in the face of separatist Francophone movements, were hardly the acts of a coldly dispassionate leader. He was very driven in this regard. Passionately driven.

SO IS REASON NECESSARY?

Well, it could be—especially when passions are inflamed by situations where the stakes are elevated. Take the aftermath of the last U.S. presidential election. The "patriots" who stormed the U.S. Capitol on January 6, 2020, were certainly passionate. To varying degrees, they bought into a bald-faced lie: that their democracy was in peril because a bunch of Democrats had found a way to game the system, when they weren't busy running a child sex ring out of a Washington, D.C., pizza parlour.

Egged on by right-wing media, the protestors swarmed the Capitol looking to overturn a free and fair election. But reason—a dark, conniving kind of reason—factored into decisions by the Republican lawmakers to nourish blatant lies for their own political gain. In this case, the passion of the mob was dangerous. But equally dangerous? The politicians who coldly saw an opening in the other team's line and moved to rush through it, regardless of the implications

> **It can be a scary thing. Having passion feels like you have rocket fuel that other people don't have.**
>
> —EMILY KELSALL

for their own democracy.

In this case, passion was actually leveraged by cynical political calculation, the Machiavellian side of reason or rational thought. The Big Lie in service of partisan politics.

SO WHAT ARE YOU SAYING? THAT WE SHOULD ALWAYS BE SKEPTICAL OF POLITICAL PASSION?

Not at all. Look, while political passion can be dangerous or misdirected, it is also natural and *necessary*. Without it, the Jim Crow South would likely still be a going concern, as would the apartheid government of South Africa. The collapse of both in the face of largely non-violent opposition speaks volumes about how ordinary people, driven by passion for a just cause, can be agents for positive change.

So how to harness passion in a way that moves things forward? We must promote knowledge and nurture a healthy skepticism—not cynicism. If passion is informed by *wisdom*, it's an antidote to the kind of toxicity we're seeing on the political front lately. And once again, it may come down to how your passion manifests.

REALLY? HOW?

Years before QAnon or the Proud Boys were a blip on anyone's radar, this topic was also part of Robert Vallerand's research. In a 2007 study that predates the recent nonsense in the U.S., his team found that when advocating for a political cause, "harmonious passion was positively related to acceptable behaviours," while the opposite was true of those whose passion was "obsessive." Obsessive passion was connected to extreme political actions and subversion. "In the end, the end justifies the means, and obsessively passionate individuals may engage in extreme behaviours in order to reach their goal," they wrote.

But in my opinion, "obsessive" can be in the eye of the beholder. Again, I believe that there is a passionate spectrum.

CAN YOU GIVE AN EXAMPLE?

Sure. We had a chance to talk with Emily Kelsall, a young Vancouver-based political activist, a little while ago. From the time she was just a child, Emily has been passionate about the environment. By the age of 16 she was making presentations about climate change in front of the West Vancouver City Council—an extraordinary feat for someone so young.

By the time you read this, Emily will be out of jail.

> **EMILY KELSALL:** The Activist
>
> **BORN:** January 4, 1998
>
> **PASSION:** To stop climate change and save the planet
>
> **CLAIM TO FAME:** Environmental activist
>
> **WORDS OF WISDOM:** "I felt proud to be a part of a lineage of activists who had gone to jail for things that they believe in."

JAIL? WHAT WAS SHE IN FOR?

She could have been inside for a whole lot of things. For instance, for a year's worth of tree-sitting, in defiance of an injunction. Or for what was perhaps her most memorable action: in November of 2022, she was arrested for gluing her hand to the wall of the Vancouver Art Gallery, after she and a colleague splashed maple syrup all over an Emily Carr painting.

WHAT? SHE DEFACED A PRICELESS WORK OF ART?

Well—no, she didn't. Before pulling the stunt, they checked to make sure the painting was safely behind glass so no damage would be done to it. But whatever you might think of her methods, you cannot argue with the passion and commitment this young woman shows. Emily did this to raise awareness of climate change, and it worked. The Vancouver Art Gallery protest became one of the lead stories in the national news.

> **Climate change used to scare the crap out of me. I would really hope and pray that it wasn't real. I'd Google "climate change hoax" on my little iPod Touch, that sort of thing. I was super scared of it. I think I've always been an activist. When I was in kindergarten, apparently, I created a petition to save the trees.**
>
> —CLIMATE-CHANGE ACTIVIST EMILY KELSALL, ON THE ORIGINS OF HER PASSION

But what sent her behind bars was an act of civil disobedience related to a British Columbia pipeline protest. A satire, really.

WHAT DID SHE DO?

It was part of an ongoing campaign against the Trans Mountain Expansion project, an extension of an existing pipeline that will run from Edmonton, Alberta, through the interior of British Columbia and terminate at the port of Burnaby, B.C., just east of Vancouver. Currently, the pipeline can carry 300,000 barrels of oil a day. When the expansion is complete, its capacity will triple. And with it, many think, so too will the potential for an environmental disaster in B.C.

WHAT DID EMILY DO TO GET ARRESTED?

Well, she and a friend dressed up like dinosaurs and played badminton.

WHAT? HOW IS THAT ILLEGAL?

I'll let Emily explain.

"I wanted to do something, to find a creative way to be involved with activism that maybe brought some of my creativity or levity to the situation," she says. "I came up with this concept called 'T-Rex against TMX,' where we'd dress up in giant inflatable T-Rex costumes and go obstruct [pipeline] work."

She did it once and got off with a warning. But the second time? A different outcome.

"The second time, we hopped the fence into their worksite," says Emily. "I felt like a debutante at a ball: I was in my giant T-Rex suit walking down these rickety steps to the worksite where all the workers were looking up at us." Then Emily and the friend who had accompanied her began… playing badminton. It was all for the camera, of course.

One of the workers waved at them. Emily and her friend waved back. On closer inspection, though, they saw that he wasn't just

> **I found I was going to jail, and my parents were obviously not super happy about that. I was happy about it. I felt proud to be part of a lineage of activists who had gone to jail for things that they believe in, from the suffragettes to the Freedom Riders to just so many great movements. People were going to jail for important things. I didn't feel bad about it at all.**
>
> **—EMILY KELSALL**

waving at them—he was waving *something* at them. In his hand was a piece of paper. It was an injunction. "He said, 'Just so you know, the police are on their way, and if you try to leave, we will stop you. We will physically stop you.' Then I said to my friend, 'We should run.'"

They started running in their T-Rex costumes and leaped over a fence. But the police were already there waiting on the other side. And that was what landed Emily in jail. She was sentenced to a month in prison in January 2023.

THAT'S HILARIOUS, IN A CARTOONISH KIND OF WAY. BUT IT CERTAINLY SPEAKS OF COMMITMENT TO A CAUSE.

Correct. And while the outcome itself may have been less than desirable—at least for Emily's parents, I'm sure—the fact that Emily herself is perfectly fine with going to jail for her beliefs doesn't seem at all "obsessive" to me. It meshes perfectly with her activist spirit. Her actions move the needle on the climate-change discussion and put it front and centre through media coverage. Plus, nothing and nobody was damaged or hurt, which is what makes for good political theatre. All told, that's about as harmoniously passionate as it gets.

DOES EVERYONE HAVE PASSION INSIDE THEM?

I believe so, yes.

SO BASICALLY, IT DOESN'T MATTER WHO YOU ARE OR WHERE YOU COME FROM, WE ALL HAVE THE POTENTIAL TO UNLEASH THE SAME KIND OF PASSION?

Hmm. That's a slightly different question. Passion is not static. It can change over time, and it can vary across individuals. I'm theorizing here, but in my opinion, it can also change across cultures.

HOW SO? IN WHAT WAY DOES CULTURE ENTER INTO IT?

Just as there are differences across people, there seem to be differences across cultures, as well as time and place. For example, some societies place more emphasis on pursuing your passion than others. A sociologist would probably point to certain social forces that could affect people's ability to pursue their passions.

Let's say you've got a passion for entrepreneurship. However, you also happen to live in the former Soviet Union at the height of the Cold War—a highly structured socialist society where "capitalism" is a dirty word. In this case, declaring that you are an entrepreneur would be a subversive act and would be interpreted as going against the values of the state. Your passion would still exist, but pursuing it would be very difficult. It would likely not come to fruition.

> **He only employs his passion who can make no use of his reason.**
>
> —MARCUS TULLIUS CICERO

There are many other examples.

FOR INSTANCE?

An economist might examine how financial pressure relates to a person's ability to pursue their passion. This is obvious, but if you live in a place where your immediate concern—your *existential* concern—is getting enough food to stop yourself from starving, or securing a place to sleep, then you will likely have to backburner your passion until your immediate critical needs are met. Think of Maslow's Hierarchy of Needs. At the base, there are food, clothing, and shelter: the necessities of life. It's only as you move up toward the top of the pyramid and finally reach the peak, "self-actualization," that indulging your passion would be appropriate.

So while you may have a passion for, say, dancing your way through Juilliard, you might not pursue that passion until you're in a position to act on your more advanced psychological or spiritual needs.

> "In indigenous communities, there is very much a presence and a practice of interconnectedness. When we all are great and thriving, that is when we internally will also grow and thrive. We are very much interconnected.
>
> —ERICA MCLEAN, INDIGENOUS COMMUNITY ADVOCATE, AUTHOR, SCHOOL BOARD TRUSTEE

But we've been talking about the individual. We should not forget how culture can be a force that shapes the way passion presents itself.

ARE YOU SAYING THAT SOME CULTURES ARE MORE PASSIONATE THAN OTHERS?

I'd hate to put it that way. Passionate people exist and have existed everywhere, regardless of time, place, or culture. But some cultures place less emphasis on self-actualization, to use the Maslow term, than others. When it comes to passion, I strongly believe that there are cross-cultural differences. That's not to say that there isn't variation across the individuals that make up the culture; on the whole, though, certain societies may emphasize behaviours that are meant to strengthen and advance the group, as opposed to the individual.

In other words, some cultures have a more collectivist vision, while others are more individualistic.

CAN YOU GIVE ME AN EXAMPLE?

I'm usually not one to generalize, but for our purposes, I'll give it a try. For example, because of the way society has developed in Japan, there is more of an emphasis on sacrifice in service of the nation, as opposed to sacrifice in pursuit of individual dreams. Shame—basically, public judgement of acts that deviate from societal norms—is a prominent social force, and "colouring outside the lines," culturally speaking, is not encouraged. You could argue that the old concept of *hara-kiri*, or honour suicide by sword, fits into this mold.

That said, not every person in Japan buys into this. Like all nations, Japan produces outliers like, say, Yoko Ono. No matter what you may think of her work, this is a woman who has dedicated her life to the passionate pursuit of art. Some would argue that Ono's mere existence is the exception that proves the rule, but this is debatable. In Japan, there are many iconoclasts.

> **The sooner you put energy into what you need to do, the sooner you build the experience.**
>
> —JOHN BRINK

Another example, and one that's closer to home, might be found within Canada's Indigenous community. It could be argued that because of the trauma that has been inflicted on this culture, and because its roots are generally much more collectivist than, say, those of the European settlers who took their land, there is more of an emphasis on community goals than on individual accomplishment.

SO FIRST NATIONS COMMUNITIES ARE MORE ABOUT...WELL, COMMUNITY?

I think there's some truth to this. For instance, take my friend Erica McLean. Erica is an extraordinarily gifted and articulate young First Nations woman. She has spent much of her life working in education, and today, after shifting gears, she is now embarking on a new life chapter as an elected school trustee. Oh, and author: in 2022, Erica released her amazing memoir, *From the Rez to the Mountaintop*. I couldn't think of anyone better positioned to make a positive difference.

> **ERICA MCLEAN:** The (Inter)connector
>
> **BORN:** July 1, 1988
>
> **PASSION:** To serve her community
>
> **CLAIM TO FAME:** Authored *From the Rez to the Mountaintop*, an inspirational memoir
>
> **WORDS OF WISDOM:** "Who I am, how I make decisions—just everything that I do as a person—is very much inter-connected to my family and my greater community."

Is there any cultural component to her passion? For example, does it come from a different place than many others'? I asked Erica this directly.

"I really like that question," she says. "In Indigenous communities, there is very much a presence and a practice of interconnectedness. What I do, who I am, how I make decisions—just everything that I do as a person is very much interconnected to my family and my greater community. I think that's something that many Indigenous people believe and share and hold onto."

And this is passed along to successive generations. "When we think about the work that we do or the children that we are raising, it is very rooted in and mindful of the people who have come before us and the children who are going to be our tomorrow. There is a sense of responsibility and contribution that comes with being an Indigenous person. In our day-to-day lives, that can look like remaining connected with people, the place that we've come from, and finding ways to continuously grow and support and develop that culture or that narrative—that we are all connected. When we all are great and thriving, that is when we internally will also grow and thrive. We are very much interconnected."

> **If passion drives you, let reason hold the reins.**
>
> —BENJAMIN FRANKLIN

Now, Erica is passionate on an individual level, of course. But she is directing her passion in a way that benefits her community.

THAT'S VERY INTERESTING. SO IF CULTURE SHAPES THE WAY THAT PASSION PRESENTS ITSELF, DOES IT FOLLOW THAT SOME INDIVIDUALS ARE MORE LIKELY TO BE PASSIONATE? IS THERE A "PASSIONATE TYPE"?

That's an excellent point. I believe there is and there isn't.

When we talk about a "passionate persona" or "passionate profile," we run into trouble right off the bat. This kind of talk implies that some people get out of bed, sit down to a bowl of oatmeal, and find glory, beauty, and truth in a bunch of boiled mush. That's obviously not the case. People who are passionate are not passionate about *everything*. Some parts of life are mundane and unexciting. That's just the way things are.

That said, I do believe some people—and maybe even some cultures or age groups—are predisposed to be *more passionate*. This is a large topic, and we'll get into it a little later on, but here's a question that will hopefully shed some light on the subject. Let me ask: when you were younger—a teenager maybe, or in the first few years of college—did certain injustices inflame you? When you learned of the cruel treatment of Canada's Indigenous people, did your blood boil?

If so, your passion was evident, of course. But it was also partly a product of what point you were at on your life's journey. The trick is to channel that kind of emotion into actions that will take you further. In other words, you need to harness your own rocket fuel.

WHAT ABOUT YOU? ARE YOU AN INHERENTLY PASSIONATE PERSON?

Ha! I knew this was coming. Okay, I'll bite. I think I am an inherently passionate person. I think that I have a passionate sense of justice, and a passion for wanting to build—to make a business that will outlast my time here on earth.

As we've noted, there is a spectrum. I think that, all in all, I probably lie closer to the obsessive end of it than the harmonious side. Many of the people I most admire also have similar traits. My passion has not made for an easy life, but it has made for a life that I wouldn't trade for anything. It has been the engine of my contentment, my explorations, and my success.

SO HOW DO YOU DEVELOP PASSION? WHAT IF YOU DON'T THINK YOU HAVE IT?

Great question! We'll deal with this in the next chapter.

JULIA CHILD: THE (ACCIDENTAL) FRENCH CHEF

"WELCOME TO *THE FRENCH CHEF*! I'M JULIA CHILD!"
For those of a certain vintage, this statement and the setting associated with it evoke a feast of imagery. An array of precut ingredients, neatly arranged in small bowls on a wood chopping block. Copper pots and pans, the signature utensils of the day. The whimsical introductory theme music, as light and airy as a chocolate soufflé. And most importantly, the large and somewhat awkward presence of Julia Child, host of PBS affiliate WGBH Boston's most successful television show, and the woman who singlehandedly introduced millions of North Americans raised on tasteless meatloaf and rock-hard pork chops to the sublime art of French cooking.

Born in Pasadena, California, on August 15, 1912, Julia Carolyn McWilliams early on showed none of the promise that would eventually propel her into the role of the world's most famous cook. She was an upper-middle-class child of privilege whose main connection to food was satisfying the healthy appetite she worked up while playing basketball—a sport at which young Julia, who was six-foot two-inches tall, excelled. Servants prepared all the family meals and Julia had neither a love for nor experience with cooking. Her passion for eating was another thing entirely. "I was always tremendously hungry," she recalled. "My theory was that the more you ate at every meal, the better off you were."

After graduating, she toyed with the idea of becoming a fiction writer or journalist, but aside from a two-year stint producing advertising copy for a New York City department store, her literary ambitions would have to wait. She drifted from job to job until 1942, when, like many other Americans of her generation, she was moved to help in the war effort after Japan attacked Pearl Harbor. Hired by the Office of Strategic Services, the precursor to today's CIA, she was stationed in Sri Lanka (then called Ceylon), where she met her future husband, Paul Child, a suave artist 10 years her senior. Child had lived in France and, while there, developed a love of classic French cuisine. After a posting in China and then a stint back home in the U.S., Paul Child, accompanied by his new bride Julia, was posted to France in 1948.

The couple disembarked in Le Havre, a coastal port town in Normandy, and set off by car for Paris. Along the way, Child experienced an epiphany. It was one that would change her life and, in time, the North American palate. Stopping for lunch in the city of Rouen, she and Paul decided to dine at La Couronne, the oldest restaurant in France. The meal consisted of half a dozen freshly shucked oysters, sole meunière, and a bowl of berries topped with crème fraîche.

It was simple but revelatory. "One taste of that food and I never got over it," Child said later, adding that it was nothing less than the "opening up of the soul and spirit for me."

After her epiphany, Child dedicated herself to learning all she could about French cooking. She enrolled in Le Cordon Bleu, the famous

> **One taste of that food and I never got over it.**
>
> —JULIA CHILD

French culinary institute, graduating in 1951. Ten years later, back in America, Child published *Mastering the Art of French Cooking*, a 726-page, nine-year labour of love. After she made a guest appearance on WGBH TV, Boston's PBS affiliate, and prepared a perfectly executed French omelette, Child was offered her own show. In 1963, *The French Chef* debuted. The first season, Child was paid $50 per episode, a sum that included the cost of all ingredients.

The French Chef was an immediate hit and sparked nothing less than a revolution in how North Americans cooked and ate. Its popularity helped spawn a slew of influential cooking shows over the years, from Graham Kerr's bacchanalian *The Galloping Gourmet* to the most recent manifestations of foodie culture. Everything from the wide appeal of *The Great British Bake Off* and *MasterChef* to the celebrity status of Gordon Ramsay, Jamie Oliver, Nigella Lawson, Christina Tosi, and Marco Pierre White are testament to Child's influence and legacy. That legacy placed Child at the centre of an acclaimed film: in 2009, Meryl Streep starred as the French chef in the feature film *Julie & Julia*, introducing her to an even wider audience.

Sadly, she wouldn't live to see the film. Julia Child, the accidental chef and the first woman to be inducted into the Culinary Hall of Fame, died in 2004, just before her 92nd birthday. Her home kitchen in Cambridge, Massachusetts, the setting for three of her later television series, is now installed in the Smithsonian Museum of Natural American History.

CHAPTER TWO

LIGHTING THE FIRE WITHIN

—

For all of us—but for young people especially—it's critical to nail down what we're passionate about. You certainly could go through life without having an abiding interest in some activity that, over time, continues to ignite your emotions—but why on earth would you, if there was an alternative? The good news: for most, there are options. In this chapter, we'll look at why lighting the fire is so important and the kind of strategies you can use to do exactly that.

SO NOW THAT WE UNDERSTAND MORE ABOUT WHAT PASSION IS, IT RAISES ANOTHER OBVIOUS QUESTION: IF WE DON'T YET HAVE A PASSION, CAN WE "GET" IT?

Well, that's a question, isn't it? Let's start with the short answer, which is "Yes." The longer answer—actually, it's more like *answers*—is complex and, as is so often the case with passion, a lot more nuanced than you might think.

THAT'S ENCOURAGING. SORT OF. A LITTLE MORE, PLEASE?

Absolutely. But there are many ways to reach a destination. With your indulgence, I'd like to take the scenic route.

In the spring of 2022, Salman al-Nabahin, a Palestinian farmer from Gaza, planted a grove of olive trees. This is a common crop in the Middle East, a staple of the regional diet and economy. Like many of his neighbours, al-Nabahin is an expert in planting and cultivating. In his country, maintaining olive groves is an existential act; if your crop doesn't succeed, your family could go hungry.

> **You have to find something that you're good at and that allows room for you to grow.**
>
> —JOHN BRINK

But something was wrong: the seedlings, which were healthy and should have taken root, were struggling. Al-Nabahin and his son tried to get to the "root" of the problem. They began to dig, hoping that a thorough examination of the soil might reveal the source of the issue. Soon they had an answer.

WHICH WAS?

The olive trees' roots had hit something. After excavating the site, they found it wasn't bedrock, which is what they'd assumed. No, it was much more remarkable. They had hit a man-made barrier: stunning, intricately painted mosaic tiles, featuring depictions of birds, rabbits, and other animals, created during the Byzantine era. In planting the olive trees, the farmer had unearthed an extraordinary history and an exquisite piece of art estimated to be 1,500 years old.

THAT'S A LOVELY STORY. BUT WHAT DOES IT HAVE TO DO WITH PASSION?

There's an underlying moral to this tale: in pursuing one route, you can open yourself to a completely different destination. Al-Nabahin wanted to grow olive trees. Instead, he uncovered priceless ancient art. And so it goes with the "search" for passion: often, and sometimes by accident, it is revealed or unearthed. In these cases, it can be a surprise or a gift, and not necessarily the end point of any step-by-step process. See, the thing about uncovering your passion is that even if you accidentally stumble upon it, it's still the result of an *active* process. It is the byproduct of doing, or carrying out, or searching. Think about the words we're using: *uncovering, revealing, finding, discovering*. What do they all have in common?

I'M NOT SURE. WHAT?

They're all verbs—words that describe activity. Even if the process is relatively passive, activity is baked into the search. Actually, "search" is not exactly the right word.

WHY NOT? WHAT'S WRONG WITH "SEARCH"?

Because the term implies that you're always the one driving the quest—that you're in complete control. Although that *can* be true, it's not always the case. I'm not saying that all passion comes out of nowhere, like the classic lightning bolt from the blue. But often, figuring out your passion is a slower, more methodical affair. Like falling in love with a good friend, it can be the result of familiarity and a steadily growing realization that something that you were simply interested in is now something that you are completely invested in, emotionally or psychologically speaking.

> **Find a direction where you want to go and then narrow it, narrow it, narrow it.**
>
> —JOHN BRINK

BUT THE "LIGHTNING BOLT" SCENARIO DOES HAPPEN, RIGHT?

Oh, yes. Absolutely. A friend of mine likes to tell the story of what started him down the path to journalism. He was drifting, basically. His first love, which was music, wasn't playing out the way he wanted it to. On weekends he'd perform in clubs, but during the week, he had to supplement his income by teaching through a local music school. At some point, though, his teaching paycheques began to bounce. Eventually, he ended up telemarketing for a newspaper that served the Indigenous community.

However, telemarketing was not something he was thrilled about. So he decided to approach the paper's editor and see if he could try his hand at writing an article or two.

AND HOW DID THAT TURN OUT?

The editor assigned him a piece, a very basic profile of a northern Alberta First Nations leader. "All I had was a phone number and a list of questions," he recalls. "I didn't even have a tape recorder that was capable of recording the interview." But he made the call, and the strangest thing occurred. "In the first few seconds of the interview, I experienced a sort of chill running through my body," he says. "In that moment, I knew that this was what I wanted to do in my life." Thirty years later, he's still doing it—on a much different level, as you might expect.

> **VERN MARTEL:** The Athlete
>
> **BORN:** July 1, 1962
>
> **NICKNAME:** The One-Armed Bandit
>
> **PASSION:** Arm wrestling
>
> **CLAIM TO FAME:** Championship arm wrestler who continued to win—despite a paralyzing motorcycle accident that left him with the use of only one arm
>
> **WORDS OF WISDOM:** "The dedication I had helped shape who I was. My passion helped me succeed."

Another really great example is Vern Martel. In the world of arm wrestling, Vern is a legend—and his story will figure prominently a little later in the book. But he, too, was someone whose passion was a "bolt from the blue."

It started with curiosity. "Arm wrestling was something that I wanted to try," he says. "I had done a few other sports. This one just 'took to me' and it was something that I just literally fell in love with. It wasn't just compelling; the passion that I had for it was almost dominating. I wanted to be first at every workout or training session, and I wanted to be the last person out. I wanted to learn as much as I could about it so I could develop my strengths and get better. It was an inside love that drove my passion."

That pretty much says it all!

> **I put the hours in and found colours I liked. If nobody else liked them, it didn't matter to me. They were my own colours.**
>
> —DON ALDER, MUSICIAN

WHAT WAS IT LIKE FOR YOU? HOW DID YOU FIND YOUR PASSION?

First off, I have discovered that I don't embody a single passion. Instead, I have developed *passions*—plural.

However, I discovered my initial passion early in life. In a way, it came about as result of two things: heredity and failure. Ever since I was a boy, I had been fascinated with everything to do with wood. My namesake grandfather, Jan, was a master carpenter who created millwork for numerous Dutch churches that still stand today. He died young, at the age of 46, before I was born. Although I never met him, he cast a long shadow. In fact, I grew up surrounded by him, because many pieces of the furniture he built were passed along to my father. So I was literally raised with his legacy.

One of the main features of his life, at least as it was relayed to me, was his motivation to be the best at what he did. Was he rich? No. Was he famous? Hardly. But he pursued his craft with purpose and dedication.

SO YOU INHERITED YOUR PASSION?

Well, in a way—yes! But in my case, "heredity" means more than generational torch-passing. As you know, I also inherited a significant developmental condition—attention-deficit/hyperactivity disorder, or ADHD. To a great extent, this has shaped my life. And in related ways, it has also shaped my commitment to pursuing my dreams. For me, ADHD has fuelled my passions.

HOW DID YOUR ADHD AND PASSION OVERLAP?

First, some backstory. I was born in The Netherlands in a town called Sappemeer on November 1, 1940, a few months after the Germans invaded Holland during World War II. As a child, I never knew my father. Like most other Dutch men, he had been called up to fight. After the Dutch forces were defeated, he spent the remainder of the war hiding from the occupiers. I didn't meet him until the war was over; my siblings and I were raised by my mother. I still cringe at the memory of the thunderous roar of German bombers flying low over our house, and of dead bodies piled high under the tarp of a horse-drawn cart. The scars never heal.

> **I guess the way I found my passion was to try everything.**
>
> —ALEX MACKENZIE, COMEDIAN

Yet despite the situation, overall I was a carefree, happy-go-lucky kid. Ever since I can remember, I've been unfailingly optimistic—the kind of guy who, when he sees a half a glass of water, interprets it as half full. When I was a child, nothing fazed me. Nothing, that is, until the war was over and I began my formal education.

WHAT HAPPENED THEN?

In a nutshell, I was an extremely poor student. Instead of listening to the teacher, I would withdraw into a world of my own making. Whatever lesson was being taught would fly in one ear and zoom right out the other. As far as reading went, no book could ever hold my interest, and reading one through from start to finish was beyond my abilities.

> I had done a few other sports. This one took to me, and I quite literally just fell in love with the sport. It wasn't just compelling; it was very dominating in the passion I had for it, in the way that I wanted to be the first at every workout or training session and the last person out.
>
> —VERN MARTEL, ARM WRESTLING CHAMPION

Aside from math—I've always had an exceptional aptitude for numbers, a trait that today would probably put me in the "gifted/learning-disabled" camp—my time in school was basically one miserable failure after another. I failed Grade 3. Who fails Grade 3? Eventually, I decided that continuing to go to school was fruitless. A few months before my 14th birthday, I dropped out and began to work at a job my father had arranged.

The job was at a large local furniture-manufacturing facility called Winschoter Meubelfabriek. After working at the factory all day, in the evenings I'd attend vocational school to study the craft of furniture-making, learning how to create everything from a dovetailed joint to tongue-and-groove joints. I also got my first exposure to finger-jointed lumber, a key part of my later story.

Here, I found that whatever had held me back in school—my inability to focus, for one—was not a major factor. When I was inspired to learn something, I learned quickly. At Winschoter Meubelfabriek, I truly developed what would become a lifelong love of wood. Add to this the fact that my father was the manager of a wood-remanufacturing facility, and you have the "origin story" of my first passion.

OKAY, I'M STILL TRYING TO FIGURE OUT WHERE YOUR ADHD FITS INTO THIS.

In two ways. First, because of my ADHD, formal education and I were never going to be a good fit. So in a sense, my developmental condition forced me to go to work and into a job where an interest in wood blossomed into a fully formed passion.

But that's not the whole story. You see, ADHD was also behind what I call my "core passion"—the overarching desire within me that drives me forward.

WAIT A SECOND. I THOUGHT WOOD WAS YOUR PASSION?

A "core passion" is different. Sometimes interests that grow into passions are rooted in certain personality traits. There is a link between who we are and the kind of pursuits that will resonate with us on a very elemental level. For me, yes, wood is a passion; it was the foundation upon which I built my business. But business itself is also a passion. So too is bodybuilding. Oh, and dressage, or exhibition-style horse riding, is also a passion.

> That was the time where it was like, "This is what I want to do. It's beautiful. It's romantic. It's badass. You can do something pretty."
>
> —MICHAEL MABBOTT, FILMMAKER

SO YOU HAVE SEVERAL PASSIONS, THEN?

Yes, as I said earlier. But there is a common ancestor, if you will. Think of it this way: my passions flow from a "passionate core," like streams fed by a large mountain lake. And it is this core passion from which all other passions flow.

WHAT IS YOUR CORE PASSION?

Now we get to tie this all together. My core passion is one that was created directly by my traumatic experiences as a schoolboy. The feeling of inadequacy that follows you through life like your own shadow. The toxic presence of self-doubt and shame. The conviction that no matter how well you do, you will eventually be exposed as an uneducated fraud. To sum up, I believed I was a failure. And the only way to escape this was to wrestle with it. To confront it at every opportunity and drain it like the festering sore it is.

YOU MEAN TO CHALLENGE YOURSELF?

Exactly. My desire to prove to myself that I was not a failure is the psychological "lake" from which all my passions flow. It is what made me give up a decent-paying career in Holland and move to Prince George to start a business—to prove to myself that I could do it, by myself, with no help whatsoever. It's what kept me going when, as a new immigrant who nobody would take a chance on, I slept on the ground in an outbuilding on land I would eventually own, freezing at night in the cold fall air

> **" I realized, especially in my later teen years, I just wanted to help people.**
>
> —ERICA MCLEAN

because I couldn't afford to rent a room. It's what gave me the strength to essentially "pull my business out of the ground," by sheer force of will, and what inspired me to start again from scratch when my first and second businesses failed.

My desire to overcome my own shame of a childhood defined by failure is behind not just my passion for my work, but also most of my other passionate endeavours. The struggle to defeat my own inadequacy—to always strive to be the best I can possibly be—is responsible for so much of who I am today. To sum up, my core passion is to overcome. This, above all else, is my defining motivation and my core passion, the source from which all other passions flow.

> "Soak up every experience, every lesson you possibly can. When you're 20 years old, you have a million possible lessons that you can learn within that decade. Then by the time that decade is over, if you have run towards every learning opportunity, you'll have a pretty good idea of who you are.
>
> —ERICA MCLEAN

SO THAT STILL LEAVES ME WITH A QUESTION: HOW CAN I UNCOVER MY OWN PASSION?

The ancient Greeks had a saying: *Know thyself.* I realize it's harder than it sounds. But there are active routes you can pursue that can take you down the path to understanding exactly who you are and what makes you tick.

But the key is in the *doing*. There's a quote from existential writer and philosopher Jean-Paul Sartre: "We must act out passion before we feel it." In other words, through doing something—learning to bake a soufflé, for example, or training to run a marathon—the identification with what you do becomes more intense or more important. Eventually, you could find that it is something that you want to do again and again, and that by engaging in it, there is satisfaction, joy or fulfillment.

Let's turn the tables for a moment, and let me ask you a question: Can you sneeze on demand?

NO, OF COURSE NOT.

Exactly. You can't. It's physically impossible. But what if you walked into a silo full of grain? Or a dusty, hay-filled barn?

WELL, THAT PROBABLY WOULD TRIGGER A SNEEZE.

Correct. So here's the takeaway from this little exchange: while you can't make yourself sneeze, *you can create the conditions for a sneeze to occur.* (Hat-tip to author Bruce Grierson, who raised this analogy in his excellent 2007 book *U-Turn: What If You Woke Up One Morning and Realized You Were Living the Wrong Life?* More from him later.)

And so it goes with uncovering your passion. It's difficult, if not impossible, to simply go out and find what you love, as if you were a 19th-century British detective, magnifying glass in hand. However, you can create the conditions for your passions to be revealed.

HAS THIS EVER HAPPENED FOR YOU?

Yes, though it involves a fairly layered story. For much of my life I was terrified of speaking in public—*terrified.* When asked, I would become so consumed by fear that my vocal cords might as well have been anesthetized. This was a longstanding issue. For some time, I had known that my inability to express myself publicly was holding me back from being all I needed to be, especially when it came to advancing my own business.

My turning point came in 1989, when I was asked to join a discussion with some key people in government on the future of forestry. This was a committee of top bureaucrats and cabinet ministers, including British Columbia's Minister of Forests, Lands and Natural Resources and the Minister of Economic Development. As the only secondary manufacturer invited, I was asked for my input on value-added forest products, which is what we make. Although I was concerned about talking in front of others, I figured that being extremely prepared was key. I worked hard on the presentation, mapping out my arguments and supporting them with loads of facts and on-the-ground, real-life experience.

> **You'll never find your passion if you don't go out of your way to seek experiences.**
> —JOHN BRINK

I was as prepared as I could possibly be. But when the time came for me to present, I just sat there. Frozen. I tried to make the words jump out of my mouth, but there was nothing. I was so embarrassed. So embarrassed.

BUT HOW DID YOU "CREATE THE CONDITIONS FOR A SNEEZE TO OCCUR"?

My former sister-in-law, Thalita, suggested a way forward—though at the time it seemed an impossible road for someone like me. She recommended I attend Toastmasters, a group that is dedicated to helping people become better public speakers. I didn't want to go, but Thalita persisted. I finally gave in and went to a first meeting. I was terrified at being called on. As I sat there shifting in my seat, I looked down at my hands: they were literally wet with sweat.

After the first meeting, I thought I'd never go back. But I decided to give it another shot, and then another still. In time, I began to feel much more comfortable with the process. I started to take chances, failing occasionally but more often making the risks work for me. In time, I discovered that public speaking wasn't something that I had to endure or be "okay" at. It was something that I enjoyed—and in time, grew to love. Eventually, I became a Distinguished Toastmaster, the highest level you can achieve within the organization.

AND NOW? DO YOU STILL HAVE A PASSION FOR IT?

Today, I relish every opportunity to speak in front of others. By persevering and being open to the experience regardless of the potential for failure, I had created the conditions for the sneeze to occur. And of course, the process of learning to love public speaking fit my "core passion"—to overcome adversity—like a glove. I didn't know I could develop a passion for public speaking, but oh boy, did it ever grab me. Today, sharing my story with others, especially young people, is one of the activities that truly brings meaning to my life.

> **We must act out passion before we can feel it.**
>
> —JEAN-PAUL SARTRE, WRITER AND PHILOSOPHER

SO THE TAKEAWAY IS…?

Try things! Be open to new experiences. Seek them out wherever you can. Because passions are often lurking just under the surface, waiting to be exposed.

YOUR PASSIONS SEEM TO BE TRIGGERED BY ADVERSITY. AM I RIGHT?

For the most part, correct. But that would simply make sense, considering my core passion is to overcome my perceived deficits—to challenge myself, and to overcome my perceived limitations.

OKAY, BUT SURELY YOUR PASSION FOR BODYBUILDING, FOR EXAMPLE, WOULDN'T BE PART OF THIS. RIGHT?

Wrong. In fact, the story behind my deep dive into bodybuilding is a great example of how I choose to meet adversity and turn something very negative into a positive—and passionate—experience.

Let me tell you how I started. One Saturday in 2008, while I was at my home in North Saanich—I commute from my workplace in Prince George to spend weekends on Vancouver Island with my wife—I felt a hard pain in my lower left side. Initially I tried to ignore it, thinking it was maybe a bit of food poisoning, which would likely soon pass. (My threshold for pain is pretty high.) But it didn't pass. In fact, it intensified. By the next day, I couldn't even get out of bed.

Nevertheless, on Monday, I decided I'd fly back to Prince George and show up at work. The flight was at 5 a.m. While transiting through Vancouver's airport, I was forced to stop every few minutes on my way to the departure gate. A five-minute walk became a hellish 20-minute marathon.

BUT YOU MADE IT ONTO THE FLIGHT?

I did. After landing in Prince George, however, I went to see my doctor. The kind of pain I was experiencing was like nothing I'd lived through before, and I knew something was very, very wrong. My doctor immediately checked me into the hospital. There, they diagnosed me with acute diverticulitis, a rupture of the colon that can be fatal if left untreated. It had been about two full days since my symptoms first appeared. At this point emergency surgery was my only option. I made it through, but only barely.

From that point on, I resolved that I would put my health front and centre. For too long, I had ignored my well-being. I'd been eating poorly and not exercising. I knew I had to pursue some sort of physical activity. But what? I wasn't interested in jogging. A team sport? With my schedule, that would be an almost impossible fit. Plus, I was starting to, you know, *sag*.

What to do? Bodybuilding, which emphasizes eating healthily and allows for a flexible workout routine, was the perfect sport for me. And over time—as often happens with these things—I became passionate about doing it. Today, I couldn't think of it *not* being a part of my routine. Since starting the sport, I've levelled up, as the kids might say. In 2017, at the age of 77, I competed in the Vancouver Pro/Am and ended up qualifying for the Nationals. And as I mentioned earlier, I'm currently the oldest competitive bodybuilder in North America!

In a way, my diverticulitis was a godsend. But really, I'm practically a textbook case of the guy who always chooses to look on the bright side of a bad situation. As I said, the glass is always half full.

INTERESTING. DOES OPTIMISM PLAY A PART IN FINDING PASSION?

In my case, absolutely. I think it's part of a relatively simple equation: if you're relentlessly pessimistic, it's unlikely that you'll be open to the kind of experiences you need to undertake to uncover what you're passionate about. In my view, optimism is an essential prerequisite for finding and pursuing your passion.

WHAT ABOUT ABILITY? OR TALENT? DO THEY MATTER?

> I don't think I'm anything special. I don't have any special gift, it's just that I went on a journey.
>
> —DON ALDER

Hmm. If you mean, "Do you need them for something to be a passion?", I'd say…it depends. Certain passions—let's take Vern Martel's passion for arm wrestling—probably do require a certain level of natural ability, or in Vern's case, physical strength. You can't do what he has done without it.

I GUESS WHAT I'M WONDERING IS IF YOU NEED TO HAVE A NATURAL APTITUDE FOR AN ACTIVITY IN ORDER FOR IT TO EVEN QUALIFY AS A POTENTIAL PASSION.

You know, I've thought a lot about the relationship between talent and execution. As I said, there are some activities that require certain baseline capabilities. But often, that's where it ends. Is it hopeless if you have a burning desire to play the piano but your fingers are short and stubby? You might have a difficult time trying to convince Elton John of this. Or jazz great Vince Guaraldi, whose playing everyone knows from *A Charlie Brown Christmas*, the 1965 animated TV classic. Or Vladmir Ashkenazy, one of the world's greatest classical pianists. His tiny hands could barely stretch an octave.

And many are unconvinced that "talent" is even real. In a way, it could be a chicken and egg situation: did talent or natural ability lead you to become good at something, or did the passion to become good at something lead you to acquire the skills necessary to move forward in the first place?

In this interpretation, what we see as "talent" is the end game of desire. It is more the product of passion than the catalyst.

WELL, SURELY THOSE WHO ARE AT THE VERY TOP OF THEIR GAMES HAVE SOMETHING INNATE. IT CAN'T JUST BE ONLY ABOUT PASSION, RIGHT?

I'm not sure about that. Take guitarist Don Alder, for example. Don plays "fingerstyle" guitar, an approach that involves using the fingers in lieu of a pick to pluck the strings. Over the years, he has become widely known as one of the finest acoustic guitar players in the world. That's not just my assessment. *Acoustic Guitar* magazine called his playing "spectacular," while Michael Molenda, the former editor of *Guitar Player* magazine, said he was "the full cowabunga package—talent, technique and passion." In 2007, Don won the annual International Fingerstyle competition in Winfield, Kansas, beating out a slate of amazing musicians to take what is probably the most prestigious title out there. And he has also taken first place in *Guitar Player* magazine's *Guitar Superstar* competition, as well as winning the *Guitar Idol U.K.* crown.

> "You're talking about hardships in life, and part of mine was being behind the class and being the idiot and getting sick and losing all my self-confidence. I think the pain comes from lack of self-confidence and feeling lesser than everybody else. My mom only had a Grade Six education.
>
> —DON ALDER, WORLD-CLASS ACOUSTIC-FINGERSTYLE GUITARIST

DON ALDER: The Performer

BORN: July 16, 1956

PASSION: Acoustic guitar

CLAIM TO FAME: Won international fingerstyle guitar championship, *Guitar Player* magazine's Guitar Superstar competition, and *Guitar Idol U.K.*

WORDS OF WISDOM: "There's no motive, no agenda. At the end of the day, it really is just passion."

The guy is, in a word, a "monster." And do you know how he describes his talent? "I don't think I'm anything special," he told me. "I don't have any special gift, it's just that I went on a journey." This is not false modesty. This is Don being open and introspective. Others may have skills that equal or better Don's, as he readily admits. But he's got one thing that puts him over the top and allows him to stand out from a crowded field. "At the end of the day," he says, "it really is just passion."

THAT'S QUITE A TESTAMENT.

It is. But like so many of us who indulge our passions, Don did not have an easy ride. Even the way he began his love affair with the guitar was difficult. After falling into a stream and swallowing sewage-contaminated water when he was a teenager, Don was confined to his bed. During his convalescence, his mother bought him a $39 guitar from Simpson-Sears, and that's when he started to play.

There was more Don had to overcome. His nails, which are usually a critical component of fingerstyle playing technique, are as thin as fax paper—the result, he says, of his body diverting calcium to the site of the broken pelvis that he suffered while joyriding in his grandmother's car as a teen. Adding texture to Don's story is the fact that, years later, he happened to be riding in the bed of a pickup truck with Rick Hansen, Canada's fabled "Man in Motion," when the vehicle went out of control and crashed. Rick, of course, ended up paralyzed for life. Don learned a lot about overcoming adversity from Rick Hansen.

But his real trials took place on stage.

HOW SO?

When you watch him, it's clear Don is the ultimate solo guitar *performer*. He is musically brilliant, of course. That's a given, considering the kind of accolades he's received. But he's also amazing to watch. As he strangles harmonics and smashes his guitar like it was the bass drum in a marching band, he's also moving rhythmically around the stage. The guy can't sit. And he rarely just stands still.

These are the hallmarks of an entertainer, not just a great musician. But Don was not always a performer. For most of his life he was "a bedroom player" and was extremely nervous about playing out in

> **We often think of [finding passion] as this glowing, shiny moment where it all becomes super clear. But while that might be true for some people, it certainly was not the case for me. What it really was was a collection of moments where I first realized I'm in the right place at the right time, and then continuing to learn that lesson and get that feedback. Really that feedback was what fuels or continues to fuel that motivation and that passion—that I'm doing the best I can with what I have and I'm having some sort of an impact.**
>
> —ERICA MCLEAN

public. He decided to change that by doing a few open-mic nights at a local pub.

Unfortunately, they didn't go too well. In fact, on three successive occasions he basically hid when his name was called and refused to come on stage. But he persevered. Over time he became more and more comfortable in front of an audience—in much the same way that I overcame my terror about public speaking.

Now performing is second nature for Don. "You have to get over the fear, you have to let yourself be vulnerable enough to show that to people," he says. "A lot of players will try to be so protective and have to get it perfect. I found that if you loosen up, play from the heart, and let the guitar speak for you, if it touches your sensitivity, let it go for you. It takes a while to get to that place, though."

To me, that sounds like Don is tapping into *passion*. And that's much more interesting than listening to someone play "perfectly."

> **Our passions are the true phoenixes; when the old one is burnt out, a new one rises from its ashes.**
>
> —JOHANN WOLFGANG VON GOETHE, POET, SCIENTIST, PLAYWRIGHT, STATESMAN, RENAISSANCE MAN

YOU STILL HAVE TO FIND YOUR PASSION, THOUGH.

Again, I think it's best if we toss that frame away. It implies that passions are things to be found. If that's the case, the quest is simple but probably impossible: to find your passion, all you have to do is commit to turning over every rock in the universe, metaphorically speaking, to discover it. It becomes more like a gold-mining expedition than anything else. And there is another trap in this approach: to "find" your passion implies that it is fully formed, and that once you discover it, that's pretty much it.

While this is possible, it's not likely. For most, I'd say that passion is developed. It starts out as an interest and then, after you delve deeper and deeper into the activity, it becomes an increasingly significant part of who you are. In this scenario, passions are made, not born.

IT STILL SOMEHOW SEEMS DAUNTING TO ME, FRANKLY.

I understand. For younger people especially, I think that the emphasis we've placed on passion can almost be intimidating. But that's because we've often dealt with the concept of passion in a way that is almost too reverent, if that's possible. Placing passion on a pedestal—by positioning it as a Holy Grail which, once you find it, will magically transport you—can make it seem like an almost impossible thing to acquire.

> **If the objective is to make a lot of money, you likely won't. If that is the objective, in virtually all cases you will not be successful. You will become frustrated because no money is enough money.**
>
> —JOHN BRINK

But it's not. As we've seen, it's part of a process: of accumulating experiences, of exposing yourself to new and hopefully exciting ideas and pursuits. Kernels of interest grow into fully formed loves that resonate so intensely that they help define who you are to yourself and to the world around you.

The other dangerous part of this equation is that many people mistakenly believe that passion, once you find it, means that some level of mastery will follow without too much difficulty. This is a toxic belief!

WHY "TOXIC"?

It implies that if you hit a wall or encounter some difficulties, maybe what you thought was a passion wasn't really a passion at all. It is a recipe for giving up. While passion is necessary for excellence, it doesn't mean that there won't be challenges and setbacks along the way. There will be times when your passion will ebb; occasionally, it may even seem as if it has abandoned you. (Or more accurately, that you have abandoned it.)

But passion is not always constant. It is not some mythic element that provides unwavering energy. It is, however, a potent motivating power—as long as you don't ask too much of it.

One of the better analogies I've read was from a 2018 article in *The Atlantic* magazine. The author, Olga Khazan, asked Paul O'Keefe, an assistant professor of psychology at Yale-NUS College, to describe the downside of seeing passion as something that simply sweeps over you and sweeps you away. "That means that if you do something that feels like work, it means you don't love it," O'Keefe told Khazan. He gave the example of a student who tries one lab after another, looking for the one whose research topic triggers this "swept-away" feeling. "It's this idea that if I'm not completely overwhelmed by emotion when I walk into a lab, then it won't be my passion or my interest."

OKAY, SAY YOU'VE FOUND AN ACTIVITY THAT DEVELOPS INTO A PASSION. WHAT IF IT DOESN'T FIT WITH THE REST OF YOUR LIFE?

Ah, this is a very good question. I read a lot of business literature, and one phrase that seems to crop up frequently in consumer-law discussions is "fit for purpose." This term means that if you create or sell something, it must be suitable for the purposes for which it is intended. And that's the thing about passion: it must align with who you are and how you need your life to be. Passion must be *fit for purpose*. It must mesh with who you are and where you want to go.

For example, if you have a passion for exotic-car collecting but you can barely make rent, your desire is out of sync with your life situation. The father who wants to dedicate his life to solo international travel and also wants to be there to raise his kids will find it very difficult to do both. If you have a burning desire to be the president of Brazil but have no ties to the nation and can't speak Portuguese, then I'd gently suggest you rethink your ambition. At the very least.

The key here is to ask yourself: Is the activity I'm passionate about attainable? Can I get to where I want to go, or are the odds so long as to be virtually impossible? Now of course, some people test their own limits in ways that are truly awe-inspiring. And I don't mean to dissuade anyone from pushing themselves as fast and far as they can go. But there is a line that separates rational dreams from, well, Don Quixote.

> **A strong passion for any object will ensure success, for the desire of the end will point out the means.**
>
> —WILLIAM HAZLITT, WRITER AND PHILOSOPHER

OKAY, BUT WHERE IS THAT LINE? HOW DO YOU KNOW IF YOU SHOULD ABANDON YOUR PASSION?

Some passions are patently unattainable. Like the examples above we've just discussed, there are problems—insurmountable problems, basically—baked into the pursuit. But most passions are not like this, not at all. In many cases, you can fine-tune your relationship with passion. And that can open another door. Or perhaps lead to an offshoot passion that fits your life better than the original pursuit.

BUT IF WE'RE TRULY PASSIONATE ABOUT DOING SOMETHING, WE'LL FIND A WAY TO MAKE IT PART OF WHO WE ARE? RIGHT?

Correct. In some way, in some form, if you have found something in which you're truly invested, you will—you should—find a way to incorporate it into your life. In whatever capacity you're comfortable with. And without excessive regard for any perceived obstacles that might get in the way. Take Katie Stymiest, for example. Katie is the young woman behind Caked by Katie, a venture that's dedicated to making the most amazing dairy- and gluten-free desserts. Since she started the business, Katie has gone from being an unknown baker to someone who has participated in a nationally televised Food Network TV show and, most recently, on *Cook at All Costs*, a Netflix production seen around the globe. And she's done it while living in Prince George, B.C.

> **Passion and purpose go hand in hand. When you discover your purpose, you will normally find it's something you're tremendously passionate about.**
>
> —STEVE PAVLINA, MOTIVATIONAL COACH

The point is that geography is now pretty much irrelevant. Need convincing? I suppose you could ask the 100,000 Instagram followers who adore Katie and what she does. That she's doing it all out of central British Columbia has no impact, positive or negative, on her worldwide fan base.

SAY YOU'RE STILL ON THE HUNT AND TRYING TO FIND OUT WHAT REALLY EXCITES YOU. CAN YOU CREATE PASSION WHERE IT DOESN'T EXIST?

That's a very interesting question. I've done my best in this chapter to drain the quest for passion of at least some of its "magic"—the *eureka!* expectation that passions are always fully formed and just waiting to be found as you dig around searching for them. Passions are not truffles, and you are not a pig.

That said, and as we've established earlier, you must be open to new experiences and receptive to the possibility that something that triggers interest in you may, with time, develop into something more substantial. There's very little magic in that! Not that the *eureka!* moments don't exist. But if you look carefully, they're often developed, even if on first glance they seem to have popped out of nowhere.

Remember my friend the journalist? In Grade 2, he wrote and performed a play based on Robin Hood—and got his entire class involved. In junior high school he wrote a short story that he has saved to this day. In college, he took a creative-writing course and would almost always do well on assigned essays. While he didn't know he wanted to be a writer, over the course of his life he had laid the groundwork for his "bolt from the blue" realization. So he didn't stumble upon anything. He had done the work, put in the time. His "bolt from the blue" moment was 26 years in the making.

In short, it's not magic, and unless you're Joan of Arc, it's not the result of divine intervention. It is the result of being interested in and open to new encounters.

> **Life takes on meaning when you become motivated, set goals and charge after them in an unstoppable manner.**
>
> —LES BROWN, MOTIVATIONAL SPEAKER

AND TO SUM UP?

You'll know you're on the right track when you find an activity that meets the following criteria:

> **Life isn't about finding yourself. Life is about creating yourself.**
>
> —GEORGE BERNARD SHAW, PLAYWRIGHT

- It's something you enjoy and that has the potential to challenge, resonate, thrill, or fulfill.
- It's something that will sustain your interest over the long haul.
- It's something over which you can achieve some level of mastery.
- It meshes with who you are and what you desire.
- It is attainable and rational.

If these five components are there, you're well on your way.

SO THAT'S IT, THEN?

Not even close.

MUHAMMAD ALI:
SLINGS AND ARROWS

IN 1964, SONNY LISTON, the heavyweight boxing champion of the world, was in an enviable position. He had destroyed Floyd Patterson, the soft-spoken and well-loved former champ, twice—both times by first-round knockouts. Liston's reputation was so fearsome that Henry Cooper, the British heavyweight champ, simply refused to fight him. "We don't even want to meet Liston walking down the same street," was how Cooper's manager put it.

This wasn't necessarily hyperbole. Liston *was* dangerous. He had learned to box in jail while serving time for armed robbery and assaulting a police officer. His management was largely funded and directed by Frankie Carbo, a former Murder, Inc. contract killer for the New York City–based Lucchese Mafia crime family.

Liston was a deadly serious man. Most boxing experts expected him to dominate the sport for the entire decade. But Cassius Clay, soon to be known as Muhammad Ali, had a different plan.

Born in Louisville, Kentucky, on January 17, 1942, Cassius Marcellus Clay started boxing when he was 12 years old. At 18, he took Olympic Gold in the Light-Heavyweight division—a promising start, but not much more. Aside from his penchant for bragging, his first professional fights were basically undistinguished affairs, and prior to his 1964 championship bout with Liston, "The Louisville Lip" was known primarily as a fast but light puncher who talked a big game. At the time of the fight, he was a 7-1 underdog against the powerful, dangerous Liston. The younger fighter taunted Liston mercilessly, enraging the reigning champ and perhaps throwing him off his game.

The upstart predicted he'd beat Liston in eight rounds. In fact, it was over in six, when Liston couldn't continue. Clay was the heavyweight boxing champion of the world.

After his victory, Clay publicly aligned himself with the black separatist group Nation of Islam and officially changed his name to Muhammad Ali—a controversial move that, predictably, sparked enormous blowback. But Ali was undeterred, and he went on to beat Liston again. Victories against Floyd Patterson, George Chuvalo, Henry Cooper, and Cleveland Williams followed. A contest against top-ranked Ernie Terrell, who refused to call Ali by his Muslim name, was particularly cruel: after battering Terrell, Ali paused between each devastating blow and shouted "What's my name, Uncle Tom?!" until the fight, which went the distance, was finally over.

At this point, nobody questioned Ali's skill in the ring. But if Ali had an Achilles heel, it was that his real passion, aside from boxing, was a fierce determination to be true to himself. In 1967, during the height of the Vietnam War, Ali was inducted into the U.S. Army but refused to serve on religious grounds. The anger directed toward him, especially from white Americans, was visceral. Ali stayed the course. "I ain't got no quarrel with them Vietcong," he said. But for refusing to go to war, he was stripped of his titles and prohibited from boxing for four years—arguably at a time when his skills were at their peak.

After the Supreme Court reversed his conviction for draft evasion in 1971,

> **I ain't got no quarrel with them Vietcong.**
>
> —MUHAMMAD ALI

Ali returned to the ring. Age and time away had taken their toll: he was slower, less flashy than before. But the desire to win was undimmed. Now strategy became more important than speed. His passion for the sport inspired Ali to find new paths to victory over boxing luminaries like Ken Norton, Joe Frazier, Floyd Patterson, Jerry Quarry, Jimmy Ellis, and George Foreman. The last of these was a gruelling bout that, along with three epic fights against Joe Frazier, cemented his reputation as the greatest boxer of all time.

However, Ali was more than a sports superstar. During his forced exclusion from the ring, he was involved in other fights. He spoke against the war in Vietnam and became an anti-war fixture on the college-campus lecture circuit. As the most famous person in the world, he was well-positioned to use his fame to fight for the rights of black Americans. In the process, he shed the irritating brashness of the younger Ali, replacing it with a quick-witted, self-deprecating, and wise alternative.

In time, he broke with the Nation of Islam, but he remained a Muslim, performing charitable works for the remainder of his life. In 1984, in a particularly cruel twist for a man so identified with movement, Ali, who had probably taken around 200,000 hits to the head over the course of his career, was diagnosed with Parkinson's Syndrome. His speech became slurred; he moved slowly. His mind, however, was as sharp as it had been all those years earlier when, as a young fighter, he had been spontaneously creating rhyming odes to his own greatness—a precursor to rap, some say.

Muhammad Ali died on June 3, 2016. People around the world mourned the loudmouthed boy who, partly through skill but mainly by force of will, became a beloved international icon. His funeral was televised. One billion people watched as he was laid to rest.

CHAPTER THREE

STOKING THE FLAME

—

It's not enough to simply be passionate. Other elements are key to ensuring that what you're passionate about is something that will work for you over the long haul. How much does persistence matter? How important is an end goal? What role does mastery play? What if you find you're on the wrong path? Can you adjust your journey, or is it better to "throw the baby out with the bathwater"?

OKAY, SAY I'VE DONE EVERYTHING RIGHT. I'VE TRIED A BUNCH OF THINGS AND FOUND THAT I REALLY LIKE DOING ONE PARTICULAR ACTIVITY. IT'S MY PASSION, I GUESS.

Well, first off, to me it doesn't sound like you're completely invested! You don't seem all that excited about your "passion." Let's review. Does it resonate with you on an emotional level? Does it fit with your life and your values? Are you acquiring the skills necessary to engage in it on a meaningful level? Is it something that has become almost inextricably part of who you are or who you aspire to be? Are you wholly invested in the outcome? Or, is the possibility at least there?

And finally, is it something you're committed to—a pursuit that potentially compels you to engage in it over a significant amount of time?

> **Your work is going to fill a large part of your life, and the only way to be truly satisfied is to do what you believe is great work. And the only way to do great work is to love what you do. If you haven't found it yet, keep looking. Don't settle. As with all matters of the heart, you'll know when you find it.**
>
> —STEVE JOBS, APPLE CEO

I THINK THE LATTER IS WHAT CONCERNS ME. SOMETIMES I'M REALLY INTO IT, AND OTHER TIMES, IT'S—I DON'T KNOW. NOT "MEH," EXACTLY. BUT SOMETIMES I FEEL AS IF I'M GOING THROUGH THE MOTIONS. IT DOESN'T SEEM AS EXCITING AS IT FIRST DID.

Part of the reason that I wrote this book is to demystify passion.

Not to diminish it in any way, but to normalize the process and ensure that your expectations align with reality. I firmly believe that nurturing a mystique about a valuable and natural human process is counterproductive to actually making it work for us. Passion is not manna from heaven; it is not delivered by gods or angels. It is the result of being open to new things and embracing pursuits that move us. Nobody is being anointed here.

True passion, by definition, is something that is sustained over time. But we all have times when our passion ebbs. This is normal. The intensity of our attachment can waver. Again, I have to stress: this is normal. This life is a journey. Along the way, there will be forks in the road, and there will be hills and valleys. And, hopefully, a summit or two.

I THINK THAT'S PART OF MY PROBLEM: I DON'T THINK I HAVE A MOUNTAINTOP IN MY SIGHTS. DO YOU NEED A GOAL?

This is an excellent question. I think that goals are critically important. No matter how challenging, you must have an objective in sight to give it all you have and then some.

When I mention a goal, I'm not necessarily talking about something static, although it can be. Instead, it's something to move towards. Goals are markers, ways of charting your progress as you dive more deeply into your passion. For example, as part of a quest to become better, an artist may strive to represent the physiology of the human hand in the most accurate manner possible. An industrial engineer might spend years learning about *kanso*, the Japanese study of design simplicity, with the end goal of trying to incorporate principles of stripped-down elegance into a bit of computer hardware—the real target of his or her passion.

Baked into passion's purpose is the idea that we are moving forward, mastering certain aspects of our chosen activity in the hope that we will arrive at the next stop on the journey. And then, to move forward from there.

Goals are not static, and neither are goalposts.

OKAY, BUT WHAT'S MORE IMPORTANT: THE JOURNEY, OR THE DESTINATION?

They are not separate. In fact, I like to think of them as symbiotic: the destination grows out of the journey, which in turn can alter the route. Or the opposite can also be true, with the journey growing out of the destination—although this is arguably less common.

HOW CAN THAT EVEN BE? DON'T YOU NEED TO KNOW WHERE YOU'RE GOING?

Aha! It seems you're grasping the fact that goals are a big part of the overall picture. Yes, you do need to know where you're going—but this can often change along the way. Again, goals are not etched indelibly in stone. They are highway markers, points along the way.

Sometimes the goals can inform the journey—the pursuit, or the passion—in ways that significantly change what you'd originally planned on doing. For example, if your passion is "hot-rodding cars"—do we even use that term today?—

> **He was a kid willing to make the sacrifices necessary to achieve something worthwhile in sports. I realized it was almost impossible to discourage him. He was easily the hardest worker of any kid I ever taught.**
>
> —JOE MARTIN, BOXING TRAINER, ON MUHAMMAD ALI

you may start off replacing a suspension, or dropping in a new engine, or modifying an existing engine with a turbo. Perhaps you've decided to make a career out of modifying cars, since you've that determined this is something you love.

But wait. In order to see whether your mods will have the desired effect, maybe you book a turn around a test track to give your souped-up machine a real-world workout. From the moment you open it up and round a corner into a flat-out stretch, something grabs you. In an instant, you realize that what you really want to do is *drive cars at unbelievably high speeds.*

> **"Our goals can only be reached through a vehicle of a plan, in which we must fervently believe, and upon which we must vigorously act. There is no other route to success.**
> —PABLO PICASSO, ARTIST

Your career so far has led up to this moment. You've put in countless hours working with cars. You've enjoyed doing everything you can do to make them go faster, faster. You always assumed your destination was to become the best hot-rodder you could possibly be. But as you journey towards what you think is your goal, you've discovered that your real journey means you'll have to veer off course.

Your real passion has revealed itself in the course of pursuing your passion. Which, because of the journey itself, has been altered. You're on a new track now. But your initial goal was what drove you forward. Okay, enough with the puns!

CAN YOU GIVE ME A REAL-WORLD EXAMPLE OF WHERE SETTING GOALS RESULTED IN A NEW PASSION?

Absolutely. Earlier we briefly talked about filmmaker Michael Mabbott. Michael was born and raised in Edmonton, Alberta, and introduced by his parents to the arts when he was very young. He remembers, "Edmonton was such a lovely town to grow up in, in terms of cultural things like the symphony and the theatre and the opera, even though I was dragged there, probably unwillingly, by my parents." Opera was an epiphany: the mix of music, story, and performance really had an impact. "I feel like the seeds were planted very, very early."

> **What keeps me going is goals.**
> —MUHAMMAD ALI, BOXING LEGEND

But you have to choose what and who you want to be. Michael decided he was a writer. With good reason. By the time he was in his late teens, he was writing feature articles for *The Bullet*, the local alternative-weekly arts and entertainment newspaper. He also worked as a staff writer for a small publication. But his real passion, he thought, was writing short stories. In his first or second year of university, he managed to land a $3,500 writing grant from the Alberta government. He wrote a short story called "23 Bucks and a Cracked Melon," which was published by a magazine that's no longer in business. "A friend read it and said, 'Would you be interested in doing that as a film?'"

He was in.

AND WHAT HAPPENED THEN?

On the film shoot, he fell in love with the process. Right from the first day on the set, he was smitten. "To see what is being born out of your words, and what then comes alive—it's incredible." It was an epiphany that had been years in the making. "It's like, 'This is everything,'" he says.

Alex Mackenzie

All I had in my pocket when I arrived in
Canada in 1965 was $25.47

Boarding a private flight with my wife, Sharon. Flying has
been a passion of mine since I was a young boy

Brink Forest Products was incorporated in 1975

Dana Meise

Dr. Tracey Lotze wrote the foreword to
ADHD Unlocked, my second book

Dressage is one of my favourite and
most enjoyable passions

Erica McLean

Jim Good at Goodsir Nature Park

Katie Stymiest

Lumber that's ready to be shipped at
Brink Forest Products

Proud to be the oldest nationally-ranked
body builder in North America

Recording an episode of the On The Brink
Podcast with Chief Dolleen Logan

Standing on the Nechako River in Prince
George, British Columbia

Typical-looking office of an ADHDer

Vern Martel

Up till that point, Michael had only thought of himself as a writer. After experiencing the profound impact that film could have on his words, he saw himself in a new light: as a budding filmmaker, a director and producer, not just someone who provides the story.

And this new role fit perfectly. Writing is a solitary act, as I can attest. But filmmaking? It's social, cooperative. For Michael, whose psychological makeup includes both strong "solitary genes" and "social genes" components, it was an excellent fit and covered all bases. And of course, that's another one of our mantras: your passion must mesh with who you are. And Michael's did.

> **If you set your goals ridiculously high and it's a failure, you will fail above everyone else's success.**
>
> —JAMES CAMERON, DIRECTOR

I DON'T RECALL *23 BUCKS AND A CRACKED MELON*, FRANKLY.

It was a short film funded by CTV, the Canadian national television network, that never went anywhere. But it opened the creative floodgates for Michael. He went on to make his first feature film, *The Life and Hard Times of Guy Terrifico*, a mockumentary based on a fictional country musician. In addition to writing the script, Michael also produced the movie, and through sheer determination he somehow wrangled musical legends like Kris Kristofferson, Merle Haggard, Ronnie Hawkins, and Levon Helm to appear in the film. He did it by himself, working out of a modest apartment in an old three-storey walkup in East Vancouver.

And that's not all. Music was also a big part of the story. With Matt Murphy, a member of the Canadian alt-rock band Flashing Lights,

Michael also wrote all the songs that made it into the film. Incredible! He was rewarded for his efforts. *The Life and Hard Times of Guy Terrifico* received the Best Canadian First Feature award at the 2005 Toronto International Film Festival. Oh, and in 2006 he and Matt Murphy were also nominated for two Genies, Canada's Oscars, for Best Original Song.

THAT IS IMPRESSIVE.

Michael is a case study in how shifting goals can redirect your passions, and how exploring one route can radically alter your final destination. His goals grew out of his journey, and his passion, from writing short stories to making films, changed.

> **It always seems impossible until it is done.**
>
> —NELSON MANDELA, ANTI-APARTHEID ICON

But this is important: Michael's core passion is *storytelling*. The medium has changed, but what drives him is very much the same as it was when he was a teenager. He still loves writing and making film and television today, as you might expect. Because that's what storytellers do.

IF THE GOAL IS SO IMPORTANT, THEN WHAT HAPPENS IF YOU ACTUALLY ACHIEVE IT? IS THAT IT? GAME OVER?

Good point. Sometimes, if the goal is all-consuming and is difficult to achieve, it can even become an albatross.

COULD YOU ELABORATE?

Let me tell you the story of Dana Meise. Dana is an amazing guy. In 2008, he decided to walk the entire length of the Trans Canada Trail. He did it partly to honour his father, who had suffered a stroke and was unable to walk, and partly because he had always been intrigued by the sheer enormity of the challenge. If you're not familiar with the route, let me add that this is an epic undertaking.

DANA MEISE: The Explorer

BORN: July 30, 1974

PASSION: Exploring the natural world

CLAIM TO FAME: Walked the entire Trans Canada Trail, a journey of 21,000 kilometres that took him over a decade to complete

WORDS OF WISDOM: "I read all kinds of books on the great explorers, and that's what I wanted to do for a living."

HOW EPIC?

According to the trail's website, it is "the longest network of multi-use recreational trails in the world." It touches not two, but *three* oceans: the Atlantic, the Pacific, and the Arctic. Canada is the second-largest country in the world, in terms of area, and Dana Meise has seen much of it—while blowing through 27 pairs of boots—over the course of hiking the trail's 21,000 kilometres. This was a true trek and it consumed him, taking 10 years, on and off, to complete. When he began in Newfoundland, he was 34 years old. When he finally finished, in Tuktoyaktuk, Northwest Territories, he was 44, on the cusp of middle age.

He made huge sacrifices. Relationships were impossible. There is basically a 10-year hole in his prime working years, at a point when most guys are getting their financial act together, or at least on the road to it. Dana knew this,

> **Great works are performed not by strength but by perseverance.**
>
> —SAMUEL JOHNSON, LITERARY JACK-OF-ALL-TRADES

but his passion to continue trumped all else. This was a remarkable commitment and a remarkable struggle—one that, it seems, hasn't ended.

WHAT DO YOU MEAN?

When you conflate passion with a singular goal—climbing a mountain, for example, or, in Dana's case, conquering the Trans Canada Trail—once the goal is achieved, it can also mean that the passion associated with it can wither. Dana himself will admit this. While the trek was gruelling, the aftermath was devastating. "I'm suffering worse after the hike," he says. "I'm going through a transitional period in my life: what do I want to do now? I don't want to do anything bigger. I can't do 'bigger' than the world's longest trail; how do you beat that? But I want to still do something.

"Afterwards, I had a lot of healing to do because my body was pretty beat up from it, my back was all messed up, and I put on a lot of weight," he says. Plus, the end of something so monumental can be loaded with other side effects, too. "I fell into depression, one I'm still trying to get myself out of," he says.

The contrast between his life today and when he was engaged in conquering the trail is jarring. "I've never been happier when I had that kind of goal in front of me," he says.

SO WHEN THE GOAL *BECOMES* THE PASSION, IT'S A BAD THING?

Not necessarily. However, it is possible. On the positive side of the ledger, Dana is still a relatively young man. But by investing so much passion in the end game, you can easily lose sight of what's driving you in the first place. Is it to accomplish the specific goal? Or is there something deeper, more resonant, more sustainable—more connected to who you are at your *core*—that's your true motivation?

WAS DANA'S TRUE MOTIVATION DIFFERENT FROM HIS GOAL?

You decide. In Dana's case, ever since he was a child, he had been captivated by explorers. "I read books on the great explorers, and that's what I wanted to do for a living. I remember as a kid, I said, 'I want to be a great explorer,' and someone told me, 'You can't. It's already been done, and everything's been explored.' Well, I was hoping that same person would've seen me on TV or read about me in the newspaper at some point," he says wryly.

As he talked about his life, a recurrent theme emerged. Although it is true that defeating the Trans Canada Trail was his decade-long goal, his real fixation is on *exploration*—to seek out new experiences, to observe and scrutinize the unfamiliar. Of course, this totally befits someone whom *Canadian Geographic* magazine named as one of Canada's greatest 100 explorers!

> **Being the richest man in the cemetery doesn't matter to me. Going to bed at night saying we've done something wonderful—that's what matters to me.**
>
> —STEVE JOBS

> **Never give up, never back down. If you have a dream, and the plan is a God-given dream, go for it. Do it right.**
>
> —JIM GOOD, CREATOR AND PROPRIETOR OF THE GOODSIR NATURE PARK

When he spitballs the possibilities, Dana comes alive. A TV show where he walks the world's great trails, for example, would be a perfect fit. "I've still got lots of years left in me," he says, mentioning he'd love to do the Camino de Santiago, the famous trans-European pilgrimage route, among other monumental hikes. "But the thing is, my passion's really this country. I have so much more to see here. I think there's so much more on offer. The Trans Canada Trail is made up of 500 individual trails, so there's no shortage of content."

It sounds like a recipe for success. In fact, it sounds a lot like the Canadian backcountry version of another intrepid television personality. "Well, I wanted to model a lot of what I did after Anthony Bourdain," he says.

BUT YOU'RE NOT SAYING THAT DANA'S GOAL WAS MISGUIDED OR WRONG, ARE YOU?

Of course not. That would imply that he wasted 10 years of his life! He has certainly not done that. What he did is extraordinary. It will stand forever as a test of human endurance and of dedication to purpose. In and of itself, this has great value.

Years ago, Canadian writer Adam Gopnik wrote about Marilyn Monroe in the *New Yorker*. In analyzing her enduring allure, he hit on a larger truth. "To be very rich or very lovely or very good is inherently interesting, since veryness of any kind is not part of dailyness," he wrote.

What Dana Meise accomplished is the definition of "veryness."

AND IT SOUNDS LIKE HE'S READY TO TAKE ON NEW CHALLENGES, TOO.

Correct. And to do that, he'll have to come up with new goals to move his passion forward. "I think it's impossible, almost, to have a journey without a goal, no matter what or how big that journey is," he says. "I'm in the process now of getting back into shape, getting rid of this fog I'm in, and setting a new set of goals. For my 50th birthday, I want to re-travel the country and film it like I wanted to. Whether I'm the host or not."

> **To be very rich or very lovely or very good is inherently interesting, since veryness of any kind is not part of dailyness.**
>
> —ADAM GOPNIK, WRITER

This is not only admirable, it's *doable*. And that fits our criteria. Plus, it's a good example of how destination and journey intersect. Each has the potential to inform and affect the other. But underlying all is *passion*.

SO I THINK I GET IT: GOALS ARE ESSENTIAL FOR ENGAGING IN YOUR PASSION, UNLESS THEY BECOME A SUBSTITUTE FOR IT.

Exactly. And it's this kind of nuance that makes the whole subject endlessly fascinating. Another type of "false goal," in my opinion, is a passion to make a lot of money. Often, when you ask someone to talk about their passion, they'll say something like, "I want to be a multimillionaire." That's not good.

WHY NOT?

For two reasons. First, while money represents value, it has none intrinsically. You can't eat it. You can't build a shelter out of dollar bills, or wear a skirt made from nickels. It's a convenient representation, part of a system of exchange. Second, in my experience, those who set out with idea that their passion is to be rich almost never see it happen. The late Steve Jobs saw a lot of poseurs in the tech industry. A lot of people got into it not because they were passionate about creating a better future through science and design, but rather to become wealthy. In his experience, that was a losing proposition:

> **If your passion is strong, then often it follows that you'll tap into your inner strength—a strength that we sometimes don't even know we're capable of. This can make even seemingly impossible goals reachable.**
>
> —JOHN BRINK

> It's hard to tell with these Internet startups if they're really interested in building companies or if they're just interested in the money. I can tell you, though: If they don't really want to build a company, they won't luck into it. That's because it's so hard that if you don't have a passion, you'll give up.

Now, if you happen to make a lot of money while pursuing something you love, that's another matter. Steve Jobs did. I did, too, for that matter. It can certainly be a byproduct of your passion, although that's never guaranteed. But the pursuit of money as your central passion? I can't think of anything shallower.

OKAY, TO SUSTAIN PASSION OVER TIME, WE NEED GOALS. WHAT ELSE?

Well, it almost goes without saying, but you need commitment. You need perseverance. In a word, you need grit.

Anything worth doing requires some risk. Usually the risk is that you could fail. Grit allows you to continue pursuing your passion, even when it seems like you have failed. If your passion is real and you have grit—that internal fortitude that allows you to pick yourself up and dust yourself off after setbacks—you'll keep your internal "fire" burning. And of course, success is often the payout.

WE TALKED ABOUT THE RELATIONSHIP OF GOALS TO PASSION. WHAT ABOUT THE RELATIONSHIP OF PASSION TO GRIT?

I believe that grit, or perseverance, flows out of passion. If your passion is strong, then often it follows that you'll tap into your inner strength—a strength that we sometimes don't even know we're capable of. This can make even seemingly impossible goals reachable.

CAN YOU GIVE ME AN EXAMPLE FROM YOUR EXPERIENCE?

There are so many. But here's one that a lot of newcomers face. As I've said earlier, when I first moved to Canada in 1965, I knew no English. None. Actually, that's not entirely true. I knew two words: "Yes" and "No." And yet being able to communicate in the main language of my new home was going to be an essential part of creating my

> **I think it's impossible, almost, to have a journey without a goal, no matter what or how big that journey is.**
>
> —DANA MEISE, EXPLORER

own business from scratch. This wasn't optional. It was absolutely necessary, and I knew this.

If I was going to interact with anyone aside from the very few Dutch or German speakers who lived in central British Columbia, I would be forced to communicate verbally on a basic level. But I wanted much more than to be able to order a hamburger in a restaurant, or ask directions to the nearest gas station. As someone with a dream to build a business, I needed a much more comprehensive grasp of English. In terms of learning how to speak a new language, exposure is key. In time, and with no other option, I began to become more and more comfortable talking to my coworkers and my bosses.

Learning to speak a new language is difficult, but it's hardly a unique dilemma. But because of the nature of my goals, I needed to write in English, too.

SO HOW DID YOU LEARN TO WRITE IN ENGLISH?

There were many barriers to learning to write, and it was not easy. That said, even though my ADHD made school a torturous chore, I always enjoyed writing in Dutch: this was something I'd started doing at a very early age. So at least I liked the process of putting

> I didn't have to go to Canada, with no money and a suitcase. I didn't have to go to Prince George and sleep on the street here. Couldn't speak the language, didn't know a soul, didn't have a job, and had $25.47 to my name. It was all part of the hardship and difficult times that shaped me later. In order to succeed, you need to have had the exposure to falling down, standing up, and a certain amount of hardship. I'm not suggesting it should be quite to the extent that I experienced it, but it has served me well.
>
> —JOHN BRINK

pen to paper, which is the first step to mastering the written word. But as they say, necessity is the mother of invention or, in my case, reinvention.

In a span of a little over a year and a half, I'd gone from sleeping on the floor of an outbuilding on the property of Netherlands Overseas Mills to being hired as the superintendent in charge of the mill's daily operations. I had a hunger for knowledge during this time, and I remember reading all the magazines that arrived at work. I drank in information, sucked it up like a sponge, and in the process began to gain mastery over the written word.

The crucible, however, came in 1975. After many years of learning, I was finally ready to strike out on my own. I had to secure financing for my venture, and to do this, I needed to present my business plan for bank financing. I had been working on the document since I arrived in Canada. But this was where the rubber met the road, so to speak.

The business plan had to be compelling. It had to be polished. It had to inspire a bank manager to throw a financial lifeline to a Dutch guy who had dropped out of school after failing Grade 7 three times, and who had come to Canada with nothing aside from a pocketful of change and enormous reservoirs of passion—and not even a rudimentary understanding of the language. My desire to succeed was the motivation I needed to not only create a persuasive business plan, but eventually land the loan that kickstarted the next phase of my life.

THAT'S VERY INSPIRING.

I'm glad you think so. But mastering English—by this I mean becoming flawlessly expressive verbally and in writing—is a lifelong endeavour. As I said earlier, in 1990, at the age of 50, I started participating in Toastmasters classes, eventually attaining Distinguished Toastmasters status, the highest level. It was only then that I actually began to feel

I'd hit my milestone: to become entirely fluent as an English speaker and as a writer.

Since then, I have become a public speaker on an international level, as well as a podcaster and author.

THAT TRULY IS ASTOUNDING.

Learning the language of my chosen country was a goal—*one* goal—related to my initial passion, which was to build my own lumber company from scratch. A ticked box. In time, this goal would blossom into another passion: the *passion* to write and to communicate well in front of others. But again, if you're looking for an overarching theme, all of my passions are related to my core passion: to prove to myself that I could overcome my limitations, no matter how substantial they might be.

I'm not trying to make myself out to be a superman here. It was all part of what I needed to do in order to "succeed"—a concept that we'll look at closer later on. As we've established, there's certainly no shame—and often a lot of benefit—in testing your limits and failing. It's part of a process, one that often involves experiencing hardship. I'm not suggesting everyone should experience hardship to the extent that I did, but it has served me well.

However, there are many stories of grit and perseverance that would probably make mine seem like a walk in the park.

YOU'RE HEADING TOWARD SOMETHING HERE, YES?

Correct. You remember we talked about Vern Martel? Well, Vern is one of the finest athletes I've ever had the pleasure of speaking with. In the professional arm-wrestling world, he's widely regarded as a legend, and his list of accomplishments reads almost like fiction. At

> **It's hard to tell with these Internet startups if they're really interested in building companies or if they're just interested in the money. I can tell you, though: If they don't really want to build a company, they won't luck into it. That's because it's so hard that if you don't have a passion, you'll give up.**
>
> —STEVE JOBS

15 years old, on a dare, he went head-to-head (or arm-to-arm, I guess) against a champion arm wrestler and beat him. From there, he was on his way. Ten Canadian championships. Three World Championship titles, starting with his first in 1983. But there's much more to Vern's story than tournament titles and success.

After his first world championship, Vern looked set to dominate the sport. When you watch him today, you won't ask why. In person, he's one of the most modest and soft-spoken people you could ever meet. But in competition he is all steel and determination, a guy whose intensity is unwavering and, I'm sure, intimidating as hell.

Almost as intimidating as the odds he had to overcome to get to where he ended up.

REALLY? WHAT'S HIS STORY?

In the mid-1980s, after winning his first World Championship title, it looked like the world was Vern's oyster. He was young, strong, and determined. There was nothing that could stop him. Until fate intervened, in the darkest way.

Vern was involved in a devastating accident. He was riding his motorcycle when he got hit by a car that literally ran over him. "It crushed my arm in 72 places and ran over my hip," he tells me. "I was in intensive care for 10 days. I didn't know it, but they didn't know whether I'd pull through or not." Luckily, Vern did pull through. But he would be marked forever by the accident. He spent months in a wheelchair, and it was touch and go as to whether he'd ever walk again. "I was laid up for two years," he says. "I had to learn to walk all over again." Nerve damage above his calves took all the feeling from his knees to his toes. It was, he says, "like walking on stilts."

Rehab was extremely difficult. "There was no real way to anchor me except to put me in a sling and lower me into a pool," he says. Slowly, he began to build up the muscles in his legs, at least enough to once again support his upper frame.

While this was a glimmer of good news, his left arm was completely paralyzed. It was, in a word, useless. Vern had won championships with both his right and left arm. So of course this meant his career as an arm wrestler was over.

Except this is Vern Martel we're talking about.

WAIT A MINUTE. DON'T YOU NEED TO USE BOTH ARMS? ONE TO WRESTLE WITH, AND THE OTHER TO LEVERAGE YOUR BODY AGAINST YOUR OPPONENT?

Correct. But over the following years, Vern did all that was humanly possible to put himself back into the sport. It was not an overnight thing. "It took, like, 10 years of hard work," he says. "It took a lot of courage and passion. At the time, all I was good at was arm wrestling. I loved it, and I focused on it. I pushed myself forward. Rather than focus on everything else that was going on in my life, I would just focus on arm wrestling. I had something to prove to myself: that I could almost be as good as I was prior to my accident."

A very difficult goal to achieve, of course. Even for someone who, like Vern, was so single-minded in his pursuit of excellence. "It turned into quite a struggle. I was always feeling like I was not adequate. To go from being so good at something, to all of a sudden having that all taken away."

IT SOUNDS HOPELESS, FRANKLY.

It does. And for many, it would have been. But Vern's love of arm wrestling was the motivational push he needed to keep at it, to keep going. It was an extremely difficult process. There were many times when he was ready to throw in the towel. "At the time, life obstacles brought me to a breaking point that I wasn't ready for." But his passion for the sport and his desire to overcome those obstacles were too strong.

And there was something else at work, too. "I was competing against myself. I knew how strong I was before. I was like, 'Can I be as strong? What if I met me across the table—who would win?'"

SO HOW DID HE OVERCOME THE OBSTACLES?

Incrementally. "First, I set some small goals," he says. "It was like huge hurdles at the time, and my body wasn't the same anymore. It certainly didn't perform the same way that it used to." But Vern knew what he wanted; he channeled his desire. "I used that energy and just focused on it so that it made everything else disappear. All the pain and the suffering that I was going through—I just focused on something that would steer me around it and give me a more positive attitude."

The passion remained. But how to move forward? By adapting to his new situation. Here's an analogy. You know how when you're a kid, playing in a sandbox watching a small trickle of water that's dripping from a hose? What happens when you build a little dam made of sand?

WELL, THE WATER STOPS, RIGHT?

Not really. I mean, yes, it does—for a while. But what does it eventually do?

IT MOVES AROUND THE DAM?

Correct. The water creates a new route. And that's Vern's life story in a nutshell.

He created a whole new technique to be able to continue arm wrestling. While his opponents use their uninvolved arm to steady themselves and provide leverage, Vern wraps his opposite leg around the leg of a table to get stability. He has adjusted his technique in order to compete. And being someone who is practically the dictionary definition of "grit," he has also mastered the mental game.

"I wasn't aggressive. I would come in with a very easy move that nobody would resist," he says. "With arm wrestling, there's a lot of jockeying at the table. You try and position yourself in the best way to beat a person before the match even happens. Well, I wouldn't give them that. I would just go in very, very *easy*, and they would take their grip because there was nothing to fight. It was on the "Ready, go!" that all of a sudden everything went into play."

IT MUST HAVE BEEN A MAJOR SURPRISE FOR HIS OPPONENTS.

Oh, it was. "I was almost two steps ahead. With them forcing their hand on me, I could tell exactly where they were going to go or what their move or technique was going to be. In my head, I was already countering that move."

The result? Vern believes that if it came down to it, his "post-accident" self would beat the two-armed champ he was before the crash. "I honestly believe that with how hard I worked and adjustments to allow me to compensate my strength at the table for the loss of a limb, I would've beaten that guy," he says of himself. "My intensity, or the passion that I had to get better or be that much more better, was that much greater."

> **Passion is not something you can hide or project when you don't have it. It comes from the heart. People will see it if you have it.**
>
> —JOHN BRINK

After returning to international competition in 1993, 10 years after his horrific crash, Vern, then known as "The One-Armed Bandit," was once again world champion. He repeated the feat five years later, in 1998. Today, Vern is a bona-fide arm-wrestling legend. If you want to see him in action, check out his Instagram account ("vernmartel" is his handle), or watch the documentary television series *Arm Nation*. They dedicate an episode to Vern. All in all, it's a fitting tribute to an extraordinary guy.

SO IS GRIT ALL IT TAKES?

No. As we've discussed, to excel at arm wrestling and compete at a certain level, you need to have some baseline physical attributes. You can't not have physical strength and be a contender. That said, Vern did an end run around what most of us would perceive as significant physical limitations. He adapted his approach, and he fine-tuned his mental game, too. By going into a match in an almost "lazy" way, he instead focused on ways to counter the strategy of his opponent, whose approach would inevitably be telegraphed.

It was a combination of adapting to his new circumstances and developing a brilliant defensive play that allowed this man to continue to beat other world-class athletes—against all the odds.

Another great example of grit overcoming what might seem an insurmountable obstacle would be the Belgian Gypsy Jazz[2] guitarist Django Reinhardt, the leader of the legendary Quintette du Hot Club de France. Reinhardt began playing at the age of 12, but six years later, his left hand—his fretting hand—was horribly burned in a fire. After the accident, he only had the use of two of the fingers on his left hand.

But Reinhardt retrained himself and adapted his technique to accommodate his debilitating injury. He became not just a brilliant guitarist, but a brilliant *technician*: the fast swing tempos played by the Hot Club required extreme nimbleness. If you watch him navigate the fingerboard of his guitar, it is nothing short of extraordinary.

These are two very good examples of how grit and perseverance can propel those with passion to greater and greater things. Most of us don't have to jump over these kinds of hurdles.

THAT'S CERTAINLY TRUE. THEY'RE EXCEPTIONS, RIGHT?

Correct. They are definitely exceptions—and exceptional, too.

SO FOR MOST OF US MORTALS, HOW DOES "GRIT" FACTOR INTO PASSION?

Grit is what you must tap into if you want to sustain your commitment to whatever it is that you've identified as your passion. It's the reserve power, the booster rocket, your fifth gear. As I implied earlier, passion is not something that progresses in a straight line. This is true for all types of passion, even the romantic kind. It changes, evolves, and sometimes it pulls back to the point where you might question whether it really is a passion at all.

But one of the defining aspects of passion is that it does, in fact, stay the

[2]While 'gypsy' is a derogatory term that is very much avoided today, in music circles it's still used to describe this specific jazz genre.

course. Actually, "the course" is probably too much, especially when you're in a phase where you're not identifying with what you thought you loved, or not as much as you once did. It may not be as prominent in your life as it once was. But there's nothing to say that it won't be important again in the future.

> **It doesn't mean that I don't get frustrated. It doesn't mean that all days are good days for me necessarily. I'll make them that way, though.**
>
> —JOHN BRINK

That's the time when you need to tap into the reasons that you loved the activity in the first place.

HOW DO YOU DO THIS? IT SOUNDS DIFFICULT.

People use all sorts of techniques or strategies to reignite their love for something. The main thing is to shake things, and yourself, up!

An artist who finds inspiration in painting on canvas might decide to switch mediums and rekindle the creative flame by trying an installation piece, or maybe fine-art photography. An entrepreneur who has had success but is looking for a new challenge can start a new venture in a completely different environment. They're still in the game they love, but forcing a new focus and embarking upon a new learning curve are great ways to reconnect with that initial rush.

The main thing is to remember and re-identify with your core passion, the animating desire that is the foundation for your accomplishments. By focusing on your core passion, and not on the rungs that form the ladder of your achievements, you'll renew your drive. That is, if the core passion was truly something that resonates with you.

Sometimes even your core passion can be obscured. Suppose you started your career making beautiful wooden bowls. You've invested a lot of time and money to pursue this love: tools are expensive, and you need a workshop. This is your passion, you believe. But after many years, you no longer get the same kick from it.

Now suppose that you've done everything possible to reignite the flame. You've tried making large pieces of furniture; you've infused live-edge wooden tabletops with epoxy. Nothing works.

SO WHAT DO YOU DO, THEN?

You have to step back, zoom out, and take the wide-angle view of your own motivations. You ask what it is that really makes you tick. Was it that you truly had a passion for making things from wood and that passion has now faded? Or was it that making things from wood was a subset of a larger and maybe more extensive vision? Do you instead have a passion for…creating things with your hands? If that is indeed the case, then the world is wide open.

You can try pottery, perhaps finding inspiration in the elaborate process that goes into Japanese-style *raku* bowls. Maybe you decide that metal is your medium. The artist's eye that you've cultivated for years through the pragmatic pursuit of craft could translate into the creation of fine-art sculpture.

But maybe wood itself is your core passion. If so, what's stopping you from, say, taking your existing skills to a new level and opening a store dedicated to making handmade wooden musical instruments? Anything from talking drums to hurdy-gurdies. What a challenge!

It all comes down to one of the key tenets of passion, which we discussed much

> **Greatness comes from living with purpose and passion.**
>
> —RALPH MARSTON, MOTIVATIONAL WRITER

earlier. You need to know yourself, in an honest, open, and non-judgemental way. From this position of strength, you can then move forward.

> **This is your life we're talking about. This is not a drill.**
> —JOHN BRINK

To a large degree, this has to do with identity. When you truly tap into your passion, your identity melds with the activity. For example, although my core passion is to *overcome*, the way I channel that in my life is through the businesses I create. My identity? I am an *entrepreneur*. It is who I am. It is tightly fused with my base desire to overcome my own limitations. It is the way I've found to address my core passion in a manner that I find comfortable, relatable. This is very important.

BUT WHAT HAPPENS IF YOU FAIL? WHAT IMPACT DOES FAILURE HAVE ON YOUR IDENTITY?

Listen, we all fail. Failure is good. No, actually—it's great. Failure means you're in the game, you're trying to move forward. You're swinging for the fences even while striking out. Failure provides us with lessons from which we take away important truths. Failure allows us to know ourselves better.

I've certainly failed. After achieving my initial goal of starting my own lumber mill in 1975, I watched my whole life implode when I discovered and exposed a scam related to how my industry was grading lumber. I was crushed, but I was also angry. I'd uncovered a fraud, one that was dramatically affecting my bottom line and giving an unfair advantage to the big players. In a classic whistleblower move, I confronted those responsible. Because of who I am, at my core, I couldn't do anything else. It was the right thing to do. I did not regret it then, and I don't now.

Eventually I was proven right in a court of law, but by then it was too late. My legal costs had mounted, and supply interruptions imposed by the companies behind the fraud had been too much. Because of my determination to expose these practices, I lost my business. But was I still someone who had a base desire to overcome? Yes. Was I still an entrepreneur? Of course.

To make a long story short, I started again. And like before, I "pulled my business out of the ground," largely through the strength of my own conviction—the unassailable belief that I could do it.

BUT THIS ISN'T EVERYBODY, RIGHT?

No, but it can be. Once you're fully invested in who you are, there's no stopping you. Or that's usually the case. There are certain people who are fully invested in who they are, but for them, that investment comes with strings attached.

WHAT DO YOU MEAN?

Some people are so identified with their passion that to even put themselves in a position where they *might* fail means that, for them, they are risking their entire self-worth. An example might be the billiards genius who can easily run a table playing by himself but refuses to play with anyone else, because the stakes are nothing less than his identity as a billiards genius. To play against someone else means to risk losing, thereby dismantling who they are at their core.

It's more than the game that's on the line. It's their entire self-concept. For these people, it is better to have the passion, and their identity, on a pedestal, behind shatterproof glass. The alternative is to shake themselves so thoroughly that their self-esteem may never recover.

But most of us are not in this boat. If you know who you are, if your passion is "fit for purpose" and your goals are attainable, and you commit to where you want to go, nothing can stop you.

Nothing.

STEVE JOBS: THE MAGICIAN

THIS IS THE IMAGE THAT LINGERS in the collective memory: a slim, bespectacled man with neatly trimmed stubble, dressed in denim jeans and a simple black Issey Miyake turtleneck sweater, stalking the stage of a stadium packed with acolytes who hang on his every word. The crowd, assembled here for the latest product launch from the world's sexiest tech company, waits breathlessly for Jobs' next pronouncement. And most of all, for the Apple CEO's signature denouement: "Oh, and one more thing"—a phrase that would introduce so many revolutionary products to a world that didn't even know it wanted them.

> **"Do you want to sell sugar water for the rest of your life or come with me and change the world?"**
>
> — A YOUNG STEVE JOBS, TRYING TO CONVINCE PEPSICO CEO JOHN SCULLEY TO JOIN APPLE IN 1983

A rainbow-coloured, translucent iMac, the game-changing all-in-one desktop computer. The iBook G3, the iMac's elegant, portable cousin. Then the glory years, when Apple pushed out a slew of shiny products that would disrupt and revolutionize the world, from the iPod, which put "100,000 songs in your hand," to the iPad and iPhone—the latter now in double-digit iterations, purchased literally billions of times since it was introduced in 2007.

Oh, and one more thing. Almost wrapped in hubris, the fact that the line never became an albatross around the company's neck says much about Apple and, of course, the mercurial man who spurred the company on to greater and greater heights. Steve Jobs has often been described as a "visionary." A more fitting characterization, perhaps, is *magician.*

Born in 1955, Steve Jobs saw his life take a major turn in 1976, when he joined forces with another technology-obsessed Californian, Steve Wozniak. Within months of their meeting, the first crude Apple computer was born in Mr. and Mrs. Wozniak's suburban garage. At the time of its launch, a computer was nothing more than an electronic tool—a glorified calculator, really. The user experience was exhausting and counterintuitive. Trying to squeeze inspiration out of the strangled language of command prompts was an exercise in futility. You may have had to use one. You really didn't want to.

Into this breach strode Apple—and in 1984 the legendary Macintosh was born. It was cute, almost beautiful. It was fun to use. Its marriage of superior function and form was also a statement for the owner: I am smart, you see, but I'm also into aesthetics. And upon its introduction, for the very first time the world could imagine incorporating a computer not just into their work, but into their *lives.* The rest, as they say, is history.

As was Jobs himself, at least for a while, when his own board of directors unceremoniously removed him as CEO in 1985. Jobs spent the next 12 years building another computer company, NeXT. During his time away, Apple managed to become just another computer company, one that teetered on the brink of bankruptcy.

Enter Steve Jobs—again.

After Jobs engineered his own reverse coup in 1997, his

tenure as CEO heralded a furious creative outpouring. It sparked Apple's eventual rise to its status as the most valuable company in history, easily surpassing old rivals like IBM and Hewlett-Packard and leaving blue-chip stalwarts like Exxon and General Motors in the dust. Jobs pushed his people hard; a few pushed back. But his excesses, which were legend, were more than matched by his desire to create products that were, as he put it, "insanely great."

Jobs' star shone brightly after his return to the company he founded. A cult of personality arose, and among the Apple fanboys Jobs could do no wrong. But in burning so brightly, there is always the fear that one can burn out. By 2005, Jobs' health began to decline. By the end of the decade his public appearances became fewer, and when he did show up, he looked gaunt and tired.

On October 5, 2011, Steve Jobs died of pancreatic cancer. He was 56 years old. The collective grief sparked by his death was tangible and universal. With his passing, he became perhaps the only CEO in the history of the world to inspire tears. Was it because he was an excellent business leader and entrepreneur? No. It was because for years, Steve Jobs continued to astonish us by pulling rabbit after rabbit from his hat.

Oh…and one more thing. Although he was admired and beloved, Jobs was also irascible, egotistical, and difficult—cruel, even. Yet, death and time smooth rough edges. In 2022, Steve Jobs' sandals, a well-worn pair of '70s-era, hippie-approved suede Birkenstocks, went up for auction. Amid a flurry of activity, they sold for a whopping US$218,750.

A ridiculous sum, clearly. But more than that: a love letter to a man gone far too soon. And a sign that, more than a decade after his passing, people are still, at least metaphorically, kissing his feet.

THE IMPORTANCE OF PASSION

—

Why is passion so important? Can you reverse course or "switch" passions? Can you realize your true passion later in life? What is it about passion that can propel us forward? Is there any real progress or true art without passion? Do you need to put passion at the centre of your working life? Can you leverage passion to "live the dream"?

I KNOW I KEEP COMING BACK TO THIS, BUT WHAT IF YOUR SITUATION DOESN'T ALLOW YOU TO FOLLOW YOUR DREAMS?

Excuse me for saying this, but you sound like you're already stuck in a hole of your own making. As we've established, one of the main components for being able to tap into your passion—and then to use it to create the life you were always meant to live—is to adopt a can-do attitude. I'm sorry, but nobody ever got anywhere by dwelling on why they *couldn't* do something. There are a million hurdles to overcome on your way to maximizing your potential. The last thing you need to do is to erect more—or put blinders on and not be able to see a path forward.

Many will use this as an excuse for not following their dreams, their desires—their passion. But to what end? I'm not saying that you should abandon your family, partner, and friends to chase your goals. Some things—providing a level of stability and the essentials of life for your children, for example—are non-negotiable. But if it is possible to live your dream without completely upending the lives of your significant others, then you should. They will respect you more for the effort, and you'll respect yourself more, too.

TO BE HONEST, I JUST THINK IT MAY BE A LITTLE LATE FOR ME.

If that's what you truly believe, then you're probably correct.

EXCUSE ME?

Defeatism is the enemy of progress. How can you pursue your desires if, from the very start, you believe that the process that will make them come to fruition is doomed? This kind of negativity is toxic to personal growth. And it certainly won't help you connect with your passion.

I know a number of people who just don't like their jobs or their lives. They're just waiting for the time they can pack it in and retire. Or they may feel they should have taken a different direction, but now they can't change course and are resigned to their situation, even though it pains them. Many will turn into very negative, frustrated individuals. I know people like this, and I avoid them. Don't come close to me, constantly complaining about all the things that went wrong. There is nothing you can say or do to add value to my day.

But if what you're saying is "I'm too old to start this quest," well, that's a slightly different claim. And it's one that I would strongly refute.

YES, IN MY CASE IT'S MORE TO DO WITH WHERE I AM IN LIFE. I'M NOT A SPRING CHICKEN ANYMORE.

> **I know a number of people who just don't like their job. They're just waiting for the time they can pack it in and retire. Or they may feel they should have taken a different direction, but they can't get out and they just have to accept their situation for whatever it is. Many will turn into very negative, frustrated individuals. I know many people like this, and I avoid them. Don't come close to me, constantly complaining about all the things that went wrong.**
>
> —JOHN BRINK

I was born in 1940. At the time of this writing, I'm 82 years old—and by doing this book, I'm continuing on the path of passion, one I've been traveling my entire life. As you know, after my diverticulitis attack, I became a top-ranked competitive bodybuilder. I started training at the age of 68. I'm trying to master the art of dressage, which many say is a lifelong commitment. Podcasting. Writing. Flying. I'm expanding my business, taking my companies in bold new directions—because I love what I do, even today. Age is not the issue.

BUT REVERSING GEARS? THAT SEEMS EXTREMELY DIFFICULT.

Who said it isn't? This bears repeating: living a truly passionate life does not mean that you're going to live a charmed life or an easy life. That's not the deal. That is not part of any rational equation. We are not baby birds, waiting for our mothers to drop food into our open mouths. We are searchers, on the hunt to uncover our true selves. We are explorers, tasked with testing the limits of our own capabilities. We are committed to living purposefully—passionately.

If you've decided it's too late to change things up—or even forgo pursuing something part-time—at what age did you draw the line? At 60? Joe Biden was sworn in at the age of 78. Or maybe it's 45. You have a steady job and a mortgage. Real responsibilities. Yes, at 45, it's probably too late. (Insert eye-rolling emoji here.)

> **I can't not have passion. It finds me. I don't choose it.**
>
> —EMILY KELSALL

Or maybe you're 25, and you've just graduated law school. After interning at a prestigious firm, you discover that you hate almost everything about practising law—you'd rather write a book, which in my experience is what almost every lawyer secretly dreams of doing but never does. But your parents invested so much money in your education, and it'd be terrible to disappoint them…so you continue on in a profession that you despise, creating a life that you're not really invested in, until you finally retire. Eventually you die of boredom and they have to pry your TV remote from your cold, dead hands.

HOLD ON, THAT'S MORE THAN A LITTLE HARSH!

I'm being provocative for a reason. This is your life. You get one. I'm trying to shake you out of your torpor and make you realize that as long as you draw breath, you must do what you need to do in order to be what you really should be!

So I'll ask you again: where is this imaginary cut-off? At what age does making a change to pursue your passion become an impossibility?

I GUESS, BUT IT STILL SEEMS...DIFFICULT. MAYBE TOO DIFFICULT.

I have two words for you. *Grandma Moses.*

Here's a woman who spent most of her life working as a housekeeper. She was 78 when she started to paint. The medium that made her famous was not her first choice—apparently, she loved embroidery—but arthritis in her hands made her hobby increasingly difficult to pursue. So she turned to painting.

And she was prolific, churning out painting after painting documenting the simple beauty of the rural American life. In 2006, *Sugaring Off,* a 1943 depiction of a rural community gathered together to tap sugar from maple trees, sold for US$1.2 million. Not bad for someone who only began in earnest after most people have retired. Her name is now synonymous with American folk art. She painted nonstop until she died in 1961 at the age of 101.

> **If you decide it's too late to change things up—and pursue what truly moves you—at what age do you draw the line? At 60? Is that the absolute cut-off? Or maybe you're 45. You have kids, and a mortgage—real responsibilities. A complete career upheaval would be difficult for everyone, of course.**
>
> **— JOHN BRINK**

BUT IN BECOMING AN ARTIST, THERE WASN'T ANY DOWNSIDE FOR GRANDMA MOSES, WAS THERE? I MEAN, SHE WAS A HOUSEKEEPER. HER KIDS WERE GROWN. IT'S NOT LIKE SHE HAD TO CHOOSE BETWEEN A HIGH-FLYING CAREER AND BECOMING A PAINTER.

No, that's true. But those who choose to make their passion central to their lives will find a way to live the dream, often despite the personal or professional cost.

> **ALEX MACKENZIE:** The U-Turner
>
> **BORN:** April 23, 1988
>
> **PASSION:** Stand-up comedy
>
> **CLAIM TO FAME:** Gave up six-figure salary as an instrumentation mechanic to live in an RV and write jokes
>
> **WORDS OF WISDOM:** "The 'next thing' isn't going to make your life better."

Take Alex Mackenzie, for example. Today, Alex is an in-demand stand-up comic. It has always struck me as more than a little ironic that stand-up comedy is hardly a laughing matter for those who want to pursue it: this is probably one of the toughest gigs out there. Like most creative pursuits, the financial upside can be limited. In other words, you're not in it for the money. And if you are? I've got a bridge I'd like to sell you.

Let's just say there are easier ways to make a buck than standing in front of an audience and trying to make them laugh out loud. But Alex does this. And despite the uncertainty, he *loves* what he does. Even though he gave up one hell of a lot to be where he is now.

HOW SO? WHAT DID HE GIVE UP?

A few years ago, Alex worked as an instrumentation mechanic at a Prince George pulp mill. It was a logical choice. He's a third-generation mill worker, so you could almost say it's in his blood. On the surface, it seemed that he had it all. In a way he did—and not in a good way. "I had a mortgage by the time I was 20," he tells me. "By the time I was 23 or 24, I had a $30,000 line of credit maxed out. My credit cards were maxed out, and I had payments—jet skis, dirt bikes, snowmobile, truck, house. I'd work all week and then after paying the bills, I'd maybe have $300 left for the next two weeks." Picture a hamster frantically running on a wheel in a cage. This was Alex.

> "Maybe you're 25, and you've just graduated law school. After interning at a prestigious firm, you discover that you hate almost everything about practising law. You'd rather write a book, which is, in my experience, what every lawyer secretly dreams about doing, and never ever does. But your parents invested so much money in your education, and it would be terrible to disappoint them...so you continue on in a job that you despise, creating a life that you're not really invested in, until you finally retire and die of boredom, grasping your TV's remote control.
>
> —JOHN BRINK

SO HOW DID HE MAKE THE SHIFT?

Alex had been unhappy with his direction for some time. And the accumulation of stuff was ringing hollow. "I always told myself, 'It's going to get better once my truck's paid off. Then I'll have more money, and I'll be able to do what I want.'" Of course, this was an unfortunate lie, one that many of us buy into. "I remember telling myself, the 'next thing' was going to make it better. The 'next thing' is *not* going to make it better. You're always waiting for something, and that *thing* is not going to happen."

Sadly, however, his turnaround was sparked by tragedy. While returning to the West Coast of B.C. after a road trip to the province's interior, his ex-girlfriend was involved in a car crash. She passed away, and even though she and Alex were no longer together, the loss had a profound effect on him. "That was one of the major points that changed my life. I started thinking, 'This thing is finite. It could end at any minute. You better do what you want to do.'"

Alex did exactly what we've already talked about. He *tried* new things, he made himself open to new and very different experiences. He moved to Vancouver and went to school; that didn't click for him. Then he tried his hand at podcasting. That was a game-changer.

> **Living your passion does have a way of stripping you bare and making you feel like you're fully coming into your skin. I think, yes, pursuing my passion has helped me gain a greater appreciation of who I am. It can raise a lot of questions, too.**
>
> —EMILY KELSALL

HOW DID PODCASTING TURN INTO STAND-UP?

That's exactly what I asked Alex. As it often does, his passion was revealed by pursuing something else. And while it wasn't designed to be a launching pad for a radically new career, his podcasting turned out to be exactly that:

> We wanted our podcast to look "bigger" on the internet, so we bought a bunch of Twitter followers. So now our Twitter account has a whole bunch of followers, and then this comedian wrote in from New York and he is like, "Hey man, I've seen your show. I would love to be on it." We're like, "Oh, sweet. Let's do this." I interviewed the guy and I just told him how I love stand-up comedy and I really wanted to try it, but I just didn't know where to do it. I was like, "There's nowhere to really do it here in Prince George, where I'm from." Well, Brian Major, a local comedian in Prince George, happened to hear this. He wrote into the show and said, "Hey, there's actually a group of four to six of us who do an open mic down at Alfredo's Pub every second Thursday. Would you like to do it?" They gave me a date in August.

He pulled together a short comedic bit and practiced until it was slick. As so often happens, the effort was reflected in the outcome. He nailed it. And after that, he never really looked back. Today, Alex spends his days writing bits and jokes, and he has performed everywhere from Vancouver to Australia. Chalk it up to the desire to do what moves him in his heart, and, of course, an unstoppable work ethic. "I really believe in hard work, and that anyone can do anything. Everyone has different starting points, but I really believe with time and effort you create a trajectory," he says.

> **It has to come from an honest place. You get on stage and you make mistakes, but if you're pushing out honesty, I think people sense that.**
>
> —DON ALDER

Which is exactly what I've been saying, too. Alex finally tapped into his passion, but he had to make great sacrifices—there's that "suffering" theme again—in order to succeed. Although I may be stretching the meaning a bit, Alex definitely has some qualities of a classic "U-Turner."

SORRY, I'VE NEVER HEARD THE TERM. WHAT'S A U-TURNER?

I mentioned it earlier. It was coined by Bruce Grierson, author of *U-Turn: What If You Woke Up One Morning and Realized You Were Living the Wrong Life?* In the book, he examines the lives and motivations of people who have made extremely dramatic, almost 180-degree changes in life.

Some of the stories he tells are classic "road to Damascus" conversions: the avowed atheist who has a religious epiphany and dedicates their life to God. Or the uncaring slaughterhouse employee who, after a sudden crisis regarding the morality of what they're accomplice to, decides to pull the plug on the industry by exposing it.

> I really believe in hard work, and that anyone can do anything. Everyone has different starting points, but I really believe with time and effort you create a trajectory.
>
> —ALEX MACKENZIE

But what was at the heart of these shifts? *Passion.* Often, the passion to align who you have become with who you really are, at your core. However, as Bruce says, you need more than that.

IS THERE A CERTAIN PERSON THAT IS MORE AMENABLE TO MAKING THESE RADICAL CHANGES? IS THERE A "U-TURN" PERSONALITY PROFILE?

I asked Bruce this very question. "The short answer? Probably yes," he says. "But it's not just about having a U-Turn–type personality. I think you have to have that and the conditions have to be in place. Both 'mindset' and 'setting' have to be right—a receptive personality at a receptive time in their life. There are a lot of ingredients that have to be in this cake for it to rise."

BUT THESE ARE RADICAL DEPARTURES, YES? TRUE 180-DEGREE CHANGES?

Correct. And yes, these kinds of highly dramatic shifts are rare. But would they ever occur without passion being a major part of the U-Turner's psychological profile? "I would say 'No'," says Bruce. "For any kind of significant shift in values, there has to be an emotional component. Because you're drilling into your own identity. You're tweaking who you actually are. Not just to the world, but to yourself."

While Bruce's book focuses on exceptional life changes—extremely uncommon conversions or changes of heart—I believe that, once again, the key to finding your own way, the way to your core passion, is to connect completely with who you are. It bears repeating, again: "Know thyself." And then, even if the road ahead is difficult, you'll have the comfort of knowing that you're on the right path—which almost invariably leads to success. And, as I'm sure Alex Mackenzie would agree, that's worth a lot more than a fat paycheque.

SO YOU'RE SAYING, THEN, THAT ALL YOU NEED IN ORDER TO SUCCEED IS PASSION?

No, I'm saying that you need three things: passion, the right attitude, and a stellar work ethic. With these three elements in place, you're well on your way to a full and infinitely satisfying life. A "successful" life, but not necessarily a comfortable one.

You see, to me "success" has very little to do with money. It has much more to do with locking in on who you are, then living your life in a way that aligns with this knowledge. Throw a real passion for something into the mix—creating a business, tying fly fishing ties, coming up with advertising slogans, making cheese, whatever—and the love of *doing* will sustain and satisfy your soul. *Because it just fits*.

If you're not doing this now, then it's time to start. And as Grandma Moses' life shows us, there's never a "best before" date to our lives. If you're unsatisfied with your day-to-day existence, then you need to reexamine what you're doing, drill down into who you really are—and find the activity or activities that resonate.

This is your life we're talking about. This is not a drill.

I KNOW THAT, BUT TO COMPLETELY REVERSE COURSE? THAT'S A PRETTY TALL ASK.

Remarkable life change happens all the time. It happens daily. It happened within my own family, too.

COOPER MEARS: Late Bloomer

BORN: March 4, 1976

PASSION: Flying airplanes

CLAIM TO FAME: Switched gears to pursue a childhood love, and in the process found joy

WORDS OF WISDOM: "When you're happy with what you do, you're going to bring that home with you to your family."

My son-in-law, Cooper Mears, is what some would call a "late bloomer." Since he was only 29 years old when he made a major life change, I'm not sure that tag really fits—especially since we've just discussed Grandma Moses! But Cooper would describe himself as being "older" when he finally decided to go after the one career that he'd been passionate about very early in his life.

But previous to this, and I don't think I'm disclosing anything I shouldn't, Cooper was still trying to find the right career direction.

WHY? WHAT'S HIS STORY?

By the time he'd hit high school, Cooper planned to become a pilot. It was something that just grabbed him by the lapels and shook him hard. In this respect he was lucky, since many of us never have that sort of *aha!* moment when everything comes into focus, at least not at so young an age.

But sometimes fate intervenes. When he was 12, his parents divorced and Cooper went to live with his mother. The end of his parents' relationship essentially short-circuited his dream. "Long story short, there was a lot going on," he says. "By the time I got through high school, it just wasn't in the cards anymore." Little wonder. The certification process is expensive. With the family and its resources now splintered, there wouldn't be any money for expensive training programs.

And the impact of divorce on children can be devastating. After barely making it through high school, Cooper was now more than a bit lost. By this point, he was convinced that being a pilot was basically a pipe dream and began looking around for other things to do. He tried his hand at a few things: a horticulture program at a local community college, working for a landscape architecture firm. Nothing really grabbed him. The problem: he had no real interests. "My dad actually

> **I have no money, no resources, no hopes. I am the happiest man alive. A year ago, six months ago, I thought that I was an artist. I no longer think about it, I am.**
>
> —AUTHOR HENRY MILLER, IN *TROPIC OF CAPRICORN*

got me to take an aptitude test," he says. The results were terrible. "We looked at them afterward and my dad was like, 'There's nothing in there! What are we going to do with you?' He was really worried."

Cooper was never a lazy guy. He'd known hard work, and he'd also known how long and difficult the days can be when you have to spend them doing something you can't stand. While the aptitude test was pretty much a wash, there was one career that seemed to offer at least some potential upside. So with this in mind, he enrolled at Vancouver's Langara College in the photography program.

SO AFTER TRYING A BUNCH OF OTHER THINGS, HE FINALLY DISCOVERED THAT PHOTOGRAPHY WAS HIS TRUE PASSION.

What he discovered was he liked it, and that he was good at it. And the course wasn't a cakewalk—not at all. "It's a really hard program, actually," he says. "Of the original 28 of us in the two-year program, only 13 of us made it through." It was a promising start to a promising career. Within two years, he'd made enough money to outfit his own studio and strike out on his own. As he was based in Vancouver, he knew he wanted to shoot for the major locally based glossies. At the time, that meant *Vancouver* magazine and *Western Living*. In short order, he was getting lot of work from both magazines, even shooting their covers. That's as good as it gets in editorial photography. He was on his way.

SO HIS PASSION BECAME HIS JOB, YES? THIS IS EXACTLY WHAT I WANT!

Except…something wasn't right. To any outside observer, Cooper was killing it. But in truth, *it* was killing *him*. "Although I was having success, it was difficult. I had to work really hard at it," he says. "It wasn't a perfect fit for me, really. I don't know. I just felt it wasn't what I was supposed to be doing."

It didn't take him that long to understand that, on a foundational level, photography as a career was not meant to be. It was like trying to squeeze a size-12 foot into a size-11 shoe. Even if you manage to put it on, the shoe will never feel quite right. It was never a comfortable fit. Cooper was smart enough to acknowledge this. "I just got to a point where I couldn't picture myself doing it in 20 years," he says.

> **I just instantly loved it.**
> —COOPER MEARS, PILOT, ON HIS FIRST TIME FLYING AN AIRPLANE

SO WHAT DID HE DO INSTEAD?

Remember his passion to be a pilot? Some of the dreams we have when we're young are easily dismissed. They're silly imaginative exercises, or they have very little real connection to who we truly are—not surprising, since it takes time to grow into a real awareness of ourselves.

But some dreams aren't just childhood fantasies. Some dreams fit, are meant to be pursued, and should never be ignored. Cooper's pre-teen passion for flying? That is one of those dreams. And so even though it would entail significant upheaval for him and my daughter, Christina, Cooper realized that if he shut down his business and sold his gear, he could then use the proceeds to at least partially finance his training.

THAT SOUNDS PRETTY IMPETUOUS TO ME.

I don't mean it to sound that way. It wasn't impetuous. In fact, there was a significant effort on his part to perform due diligence. This was necessary, of course, since he'd never flown a plane before or taken any courses at all. But he did have some connections in the industry. "I had a couple of friends in the business. I told them, 'Don't sugarcoat it. Tell me what it's like and how I'd go about doing it.'" The upshot of the advice? Go to a flight school and ask to undertake a "fam flight"—a flight intended to help familiarize a newbie with what it takes to pilot an aircraft.

So he hops in a Cessna 152, a little two-seater plane, and settles in next to the pilot. And then—Cooper had no idea this was coming—the pilot asked him to get a little hands-on. "He actually let me do the takeoff! The hardest part is using the pedals, so he was steering with his feet. But I was using the control column, and he just talked me through it. I just took off! It was amazing," he says. "I just instantly loved it."

SO WHAT HAPPENED? DID HE IMMEDIATELY QUIT HIS PHOTOGRAPHY GIG AND START FLIGHT TRAINING?

It was a little more involved than that. But in a way, yes, that's what occurred. This timing, however, was a bit ironic. Cooper had just been offered a very large and prestigious photography project. It would have taken six months to complete, and the income was substantial. His commitment to begin flying lessons, to follow his passion now, was so strong that he turned it down flat.

Today, many years after that first "fam flight," Cooper has moved up the ladder and now flies passenger airliners for WestJet, Canada's second-largest airline. "I feel super lucky, because I'm doing something that I really enjoy," he says. "It's a fun, fun job. I get to work with really great people, and I get to fly this crazy machine! Not everyone gets to do something that they really enjoy."

That's true, of course. But shouldn't they? This is the point behind both Cooper's story and Alex Mackenzie's. Deep in their hearts, they realized that the path they were on would not provide them with any kind of life-affirming satisfaction. They also knew that to continue to live a life without putting passion at its centre would eventually become a soul-destroying exercise, one that couldn't be papered over by any amount of money or "success."

They forced their own choice: either make a dramatic change and soar—literally, in Cooper's case!—or mark time until the end of their lives. Thank goodness both chose the former.

OKAY, I GET IT. IF BOTH THESE GUYS WHO GAVE UP SO MUCH CAN EMBRACE THEIR PASSION, SO CAN WE.

Exactly. To really move your own goalposts, you need to put your passion at the centre of your life. With passion as your lodestar, lighting the way forward, you'll spend your *life*—a substantial chunk of it—pursuing what you love. On a daily basis, that is such a powerful, productive, and beautiful thing. Forget all the self-help books and business advice. The most critical thing anyone can do to ensure they have a meaningful existence *on a day-to-day basis* is to choose a career that moves in lockstep with their passions.

When this synchronicity occurs, your life will never be the same. You get up in the morning excited to go to work. Your days aren't just tolerable: they're infused with energy, zeal, direction. Your life has meaning, purpose, and, most importantly and elusively, joy.

THAT SOUNDS GREAT…BUT WHAT IF I'M NOT PREPARED TO GO THE EXTRA MILE? CAN I JUST PURSUE MY PASSION ON A PART-TIME BASIS, AT LEAST?

Yes, you can. Not every passion culminates in a career. If you're truly passionate about an activity and find pleasure or satisfaction or bliss in doing it, then that is valuable in and of itself—and may well be enough for you. While some "passion advocates" equate part-time passion with being a dilettante, that's not what I believe. Nor is it fair.

People invest enormous amounts of time and energy pursuing activities that are sidelines, often performing at a level that others don't approach. It may be that for solid, pragmatic reasons they have chosen or needed to forgo embracing their passion in a career setting. That is totally valid. You have adjusted your expectations of your passion, likely with good reason. But there is another way forward.

HOW SO?

By adjusting the *execution*.

HOW WOULD SOMEONE DO THIS?

Let's bring Don Alder back into the picture, in a hypothetical way. Somewhere along his journey, Don decided that what he really wanted to do was to play music in front of a live audience and get the kind of feedback that only comes from that environment. But let's say that Don's nervousness about performing was something that he just couldn't overcome. Instead of taking those first steps and putting his name on the list at open-mic night, suppose he decided instead to just stay at home. One obvious result of this decision? He wouldn't have a career performing music in front of people in clubs, that's for sure.

But does that mean that his dreams should simply wither and die? Not at all.

There are many ways to fine-tune passion. If you're a musician and your core passion is performing but you're scared to death of stepping onto a stage, you can still indulge your dream. Today, all you need is a live-stream setup, and instead of playing to a roomful of pub patrons who may or may not be all that interested in what you're doing, you're narrowcasting via the web to potentially millions of people who will tune in, and stay tuned in, while you give a full concert from the comfort of your own kitchen.

Your passion for live performing? You've fine-tuned it. You've taken an expectation and adjusted it to better meet your circumstances. You're doing what you love—and you may end up doing it for a

> "A life without passion? I see that in people: they just float through life and they really get nowhere. They just live and survive and they take shortcuts. I pray for people like that. It's part of my passion today. I'm living my dream despite huge, huge barriers in my early years. I try to help people, anyone, but especially young people, young adults just starting out in life. They've got their careers ahead of them. I explain my situation. I talk to them when and where I can, and I try to encourage them, "Never give up. Go for your dreams and take it slow. Don't cut corners and think positively. Courage and honesty, I can't stress those two things enough. They go hand in hand. If you're not honest, sooner or later, you'll get in trouble. Put all these things together and dream big." I tell them that. The sky's the limit. Dream big. You will accomplish your dreams and goals, just as I have.
>
> —JIM GOOD

living, too, if you truly dedicate yourself to that possibility.

This is only one example, of course.

OKAY, THAT SOUNDS DOABLE.

It is. Still, I'd like to stake out some controversial territory: if at all possible, don't shortchange yourself by turning your passion into a hobby. It's far better to turn your hobby into a career.

And let's try to avoid "hobby."

WHY? WHAT'S WRONG WITH "HOBBY"?

There are a couple of things. First and foremost, the term has come to imply a lack of seriousness. "Hobby"—it's something a middle-aged man engages in when he disappears into his garage after dinner to play with tools. It lacks significance or *gravitas*. Plus, it also sounds a little transient, doesn't it? My "hobby": it seems to indicate something you can put down, an activity that you can take or leave. And to be fair to those who indulge their passions on a part-time basis, that's not nearly an accurate picture.

For example, I know amateur woodworkers who are easily more accomplished in, say, the art of furniture-making than others who have chosen to make their living this way. This is fine: the amateur furniture-maker likely gets incredible pleasure from the *doing*, even though they're pursuing it outside of their workday. But if you want to take your passion to the next level—to really live with passion at the centre of your life—my best advice is to *make your passion your living*. Otherwise, as I said, you're shortchanging yourself.

THAT SOUNDS A BIT JUDGMENTAL, TO BE HONEST.

I don't mean it to be.

Again, I have nothing against anyone who indulges their passion on a part-time basis. For example, I enjoy dressage, or show-riding. My wife Sharon and I make a point of taking the horses out every weekend, weather excepting. We both work hard at becoming better riders, and we get enormous satisfaction from it.

At this point, dressage is an important part of our life together. It's a welcome and gratifying addition to my weekends with Sharon, no question, and that in and of itself is significant. Both of us pursue the sport with tenacity, drive, and dedication. And we'll continue to do this. But there's no shame in not putting it at my life's centre on a daily basis. As I've mentioned, I have *passions*, not a single passion. Some, like writing and podcasting, are also part-time pursuits. I love doing both.

But my main passion is the same as when I first got off the Greyhound bus in Prince George, B.C., back in 1965. I wanted to prove to myself that John Brink, who couldn't manage to pass Grade 7, could overcome all the odds stacked against him and create not just a single thriving company, but a dynamic group of companies that will live on long after he is gone. This is my passion, my redemption, my purpose, and my legacy.

The point is this: you can have many passions. But you have one life. If at all possible, make sure that you put *one* of your passions at its centre. If you want to make it happen, you can make it happen!

OKAY, GOT IT. MAKE SURE YOU MERGE YOUR CAREER WITH YOUR DREAM; THAT WAY, IT'S SITUATED AT THE CENTRE OF YOUR LIFE. RIGHT?

Well, yes. But I'm going to walk that back, just a little. Sometimes your passion can be central to your life without it being the way you make a living.

As an example, let's look at Jim Good. Jim was a janitor for his entire working life: 50 years spent cleaning up after others in private and public institutions such as schools. For his final 20 working years, he was a janitor at University Hospital of Northern British Columbia. Jim is now retired—and yet, he's busier than almost anyone I know.

JIM GOOD: The Archivist

BORN: February 9, 1950

PASSION: Collecting plants (and record albums)

CLAIM TO FAME: Founded and manages the Goodsir Nature Park and Botanical Museum, a 160-acre conservatory featuring over 300 species of plants and trees from across Canada

WORDS OF WISDOM: "Never give up, never back down. If you have a dream, and the plan is a God-given dream, go for it. Do it right."

WHY? WHAT'S EATING UP HIS DAYS?

First, some backstory. From the time he was a child, Jim had a dream. Actually, more like two. "In the summer of '56, I remember going camping as a six-year-old with my mom and dad," he says. "As a little boy, I was fascinated by the trees and plants at Cultus Lake, where we camped. At the same time, I started listening to my dad's car radio and found I could carry a song in the back of my mind." When Jim was 9, his mother gave him an updated edition of *The Native Trees of Canada*, which was originally published in 1917 by the Canadian Department of Northern Affairs and National Resources.

The book cemented his life's purpose. From then on, he was hooked. "I studied where all the trees were found and learned all the names—even some of the Latin names," he says. "Today, the book looks like a worn-out Bible."

These twin childhood fascinations—botany and music—started Jim down a path that would consume his entire adult life. (Sadly, a career as a professional botanist was probably out of the question; like me, Jim has a developmental disability that made formal education almost impossible.) Over the course of many years, in his spare time Jim traveled almost all of Canada, collecting plant specimens and record albums with equal passion. But it was the plant collection that would determine his life's course, a goal—a calling, really—that became impossible to ignore. That desire was to create a nature park and botanical museum on his own land, a place where Jim could share his knowledge of Canadian trees and plants—and his amazing music collection—with anyone who wanted to stop by.

> **I was given a book by my mom when I was nine years old: *The Native Trees of Canada*. Today it looks like a worn-out Bible.**
>
> —JIM GOOD, SELF-TAUGHT BOTANIST, MUSIC COLLECTOR

In 1987, he got closer to the dream when he bought a quarter-section parcel of land about 30 minutes north of Prince George, B.C. It was raw land: no services, not even power. Nevertheless, Jim and his wife became modern homesteaders, living on their plot in a tiny unheated cabin. In 1989, Goodsir Nature Park and Botanical Museum opened its doors to the public. Since then, it has grown to include about two miles of trails, featuring over 300 plant species and 500 display pots lined along the paths. "There's nowhere else in Canada where you can come and see all the native trees, from every province and territory, growing in one spot along the two miles of trails," he says.

Remarkable, isn't it? Admission costs nothing. A donation, though, would be appreciated. And appropriate.

ENTRANCE IS BY DONATION ONLY? HOW DOES HE MAKE THAT WORK?

He doesn't have to "make it work," since it's not designed to be a commercial venture. It's a labour of love, a testament to his passion. Or *passions*, rather. Jim has since repositioned his original homestead cabin as The Goodsir Botanical Museum, but it's also where he keeps his music collection, which is likewise open to the public: over 42,000 records and counting. But it's the Botanical Museum that is the marquee draw. "Today it has over 3,000 press samples of native trees, showcase displays, wood samples—and other things of interest housed in what used be our little starter home," says Jim.

All of this was done through sheer force of will, on a janitor's salary. As you can imagine, it was far from easy. In true "passion fashion," Jim suffered for his dream. Like all of us, he's had moments where his passion wavered. "Many, many times," he admits. "I guess the lead cause has been financial. I've had to put things together, I couldn't afford to buy even basic things. I had to scrape and save and then make do with what little I had, scrap wood and stuff like that to get the display signs put together. But it all came together

> **I was born with a learning disability. I couldn't learn in a traditional way and I tried very hard, but I failed twice in 12 years, and I made it to Grade 10. If I was left alone at my own pace, I discovered I could do wonderful things and create miracles.**
>
> —JIM GOOD

through time."

Does this sound like a "hobby" to you?

NO, NOT AT ALL. IT SOUNDS LIKE A FULL-TIME OBSESSION FROM A GUY WHO IS COMPLETELY COMMITTED TO A DREAM.

Correct.

So even though Goodsir Nature Park was not the centre of Jim's career, he dedicated so much time to his "hobby" that he definitely put it at the centre of his life. This was no side hustle. This wasn't a guy who dabbled, or who tinkered in a suburban garage. This man dedicated his entire life to a 35-year project that would never bring in much money at all, but in ways that fulfilled him spiritually and deeply touched me.

In honour of Jim, I named two streets after him in one of our subdivisions, Goodsir Crescent and Goodsir Place. And I wasn't the only one taking note. In 2022, Jim was given the Community Award from the British Columbia Achievement Foundation, in recognition of his incredible—and incredibly selfless—accomplishment.

> **I did very poorly in school because I was born with a handicap, so I've had to fight that handicap all my life. It kept me from going on to post-secondary—university, trade school, or anything like that—but it never stopped me from achieving my goal.**
>
> —JIM GOOD

IS THERE ANOTHER LESSON HERE? IS IT SMARTER TO KEEP WORK AND PASSION SEPARATE?

Jim's story is of adaptation. I'm sure if it were possible, he would have loved to have had a career as a traditional botanist. His disability meant that this path would be very difficult, if not impossible. But he engaged his passion deeply, and put it at his life's centre, without any thought of monetary reward.

The real lesson of Jim's story is, make the most of your life and create your own dream. Life is uncontrollable. You can be hit by a car while crossing the street. You can eat all the right things, limit stress, never drink too much, sleep well every night and, *bang!* Out of nowhere, you're in your doctor's office talking about next steps because, well, your tests results have come back—and they don't look good.

I'll say it again. Our time here is finite. And incredibly short. Why not spend it doing what you love as much of the time as possible?

BY MAKING YOUR PASSION AN EVERYDAY THING, THOUGH, COULD YOU END UP BECOMING ESTRANGED FROM IT?

Ah. Now that's actually a very good question. No matter what your passion is, or how you're pursuing it, this doesn't guarantee that every day is going to be enjoyable or that you'll stay consistently motivated. Sometimes when it comes to pursuing goals, you need to rely on discipline, especially through the bad times. But whether you make your passion your career or not, if you don't face challenges while pursuing your goals, you'll lose out on the opportunity for ultimate growth.

But yes, I get that putting your passion on the line in a day-to-day scenario does come with a risk: you may discover that what you thought was your passion, well, wasn't. However, please keep in mind that nothing worth pursuing, even romantic love, marches forward in a straight trajectory. I've doubted myself and my passion for what I do. Especially when my business was faltering, there were days when I wondered whether I had what it took to move forward—to see my passion through to the next level.

People take breaks, even from things they love. Sometimes the breaks can be measured in years—a pianist who stops playing because they've "lost" the desire to make music, for example, only to return to their instrument with renewed vigour after hearing a new piece of music that totally blows them away. Sometimes these "estrangements" resolve. Other times you have to nudge them along. The bored chef who quits his job at the famous country club may rekindle his love of cooking by taking his skills on the road—in a food cart.

If your ennui doesn't resolve, though, it's possible that your "passion" may not have been your passion in the first place. Especially considering that one of the criteria for defining passion is that it must endure over time.

But there is a common thread in all the stories of people, including myself, who have put passion at the centre of their lives: Not a single one of us would ever change our decision to pursue our dreams as part of our daily existence.

OKAY, HERE'S A CHALLENGE: BREAK DOWN WHY IT'S SO IMPORTANT. I KNOW THE CLICHÉS AND THE PLATITUDES. GIVE ME SOMETHING MORE.

Baked into the pursuit of passion are goals. Aiming for and then hitting those goals provides a sense of accomplishment, which in turn again fuels your passion. You are propelled forward—towards success, in whatever way you choose to define it—by this symbiotic process. As I've often said, passion + attitude + work ethic = success. It's a simple, basic formula that has served me extremely well throughout my life. Again, it is the three-legged stool of accomplishment, an equation that can extract meaning from your life.

Success looks different to everyone. One writer might view writing an epic historical novel as a "success," while another writer may work hard all their life to craft the perfect sentence, poem, or paragraph. It doesn't matter. The point is that both are driven to create, and hitting a mark on the way to their ultimate goal (which we know can shift!) reinvigorates their passion, encouraging them to aim for greater and greater achievements. Ultimately, this leads to an equilibrium, of sorts. With every milestone hit, confidence increases. The urgency and insecurity that may have marked the initial pursuit of your passion tends to fade. Achievement makes your passion bloom, and it becomes something very different over time: a sense of deep and enduring satisfaction results.

This is your nirvana. This is your bullseye. This is where you want to be. And ideally, by putting passion at the centre of your life, it's where you will *live* on a regular basis.

But really, there is much more to passion than the individual.

REALLY? IN WHAT WAYS?

Okay, let's look at the big-picture stuff. Let's talk about progress and humankind. Think about this: in the absence of passion, how likely is progress? In a nutshell: not too likely at all.

The need to explore, to create, innovate, improve—all of these are born out of passion. And all are inextricably linked to humankind's urge to move forward, to go beyond what we're capable of. Without passion to challenge ourselves and the limitations of our everyday existence, the result is stagnation. Humankind is like the proverbial shark cutting through the ocean waters: if it doesn't constantly move forward, it could die.

Without passionate commitment, would Alexander Graham Bell have invented the telephone? Or Marconi the radio? Without the passion to reach out and explore the universe, would there have ever been a coordinated effort that resulted in the moonshot or the Mars probe landing? Would smallpox still claim countless lives if Edward Jenner hadn't channelled his zeal for science into developing the first vaccine? At one point, the AIDS ward at St. Paul's Hospital in Vancouver was overflowing. In 2014, due to medical advances in the treatment of this terrible disease, the ward was closed down.

Now *that's* progress, and that's what passion sparks. But this is true on an individual basis, too.

ARE YOU TALKING ABOUT YOUR OWN LIFE?

Correct. My first business was all about moving goalposts. It was a case study in innovation—a way to tie my goals to the reality of an industry that was, and is, very difficult to break into as an individual.

Initially when I came to Canada, my dream was fairly basic: I wanted to have a lumber mill. When I arrived and figured out the lay of the land, I realized that there was a structural reality in place that I could not ignore. In B.C., up to 95% percent of the timber is cut from provincially owned land. So instead of a forestry company logging its own forests, at a rate that it determines, the government gives private corporations renewable forest licences to harvest

> **I missed out on my grandpa's funeral, my sister's wedding. If you want to look at finances, I'm out literally hundreds of thousands of dollars in wages—we're talking $600,000, $700,000, which I'll never gain back from book sales. But that wasn't the point of my life anyway. A lot of people can't understand that, because for most people, it's about accumulating things. For me, it's not. It's about the things I do.**
>
> —DANA MEISE

lumber from public lands. This way, the government can control the "cut rate," which is how much timber can be harvested in relation to how long it takes to replant and replace a tree. This is what's known as the "annual allowable cut."

In the B.C. interior, the area that includes the region surrounding Prince George, up to 85% percent of the allowable annual cut is given to just three or four companies. These are the big players, and their size is no accident. In the 1950s, there were over 500 sawmills operating in the region. Almost all of them were independently owned and operated. But in the early 1960s there was a policy change, initiated by forestry companies that had never been huge regional players in the past but who now wanted in. A deal was struck between these large companies and the sitting Social Credit government: in exchange for building pulp mills, these companies would receive licences to cut timber in a specific area.

There was more. To nudge the industry toward efficiency, the government initiated something called "close utilization." This meant that to get access to Crown timber, each mill would also have to be equipped to debark and chip the harvested timber. The amount of capital required to buy chippers and debarkers is literally millions of dollars—well beyond what most small independents could afford. To keep their licences, the small mills would have had to go deep into debt. The large companies, which had already agreed to build pulp mills in exchange for timber rights, knew this. The small independents were basically swallowed up. It was the first major wave of consolidation in the British Columbia forestry sector, and it continues to shape the industry today.

With the small independents out of the picture, the vast majority of the annual allowable cut was divided among around a select few B.C. forestry companies. So how could I, as a young man armed only with determination and a passionate desire to own my own sawmill, ever hope to compete against the giants?

THAT WAS WHAT I WAS GOING TO ASK. HOW *COULD* YOU COMPETE?

I've described this briefly earlier in the book, but basically, I had to discover a niche and build my success from there. In Holland, where I'm from originally, I was aware of something called "finger jointing." Basically, it's a process that allows you to take small, unusable bits of wood—too small to, say, be used as a stud—and join them together in a way that not only makes them a proper stud length, but superior to regular studs cut from longer logs.

To make a long story short, I saw an opening that was not being exploited by the big logging companies. I would build a mill that could use the cast-off "fibre" (that's industry-speak for "wood") and sell my product to places where the integrity of a wood stud is critical—like, for example, the very hot and humid parts of the southern United States, where stud warping is a constant threat.

My passion moved me to find a way to be a player in an industry that was essentially slamming the door on anyone who wasn't massively capitalized. I worked for years on my business plan, and hectored my bank manager on a weekly basis until I got the seed-loan financing I needed to play in this sandbox.

Today, I am the largest secondary manufacturer of wood products in North America.

THAT IS TRULY EXTRAORDINARY.

I like the word you chose: "extraordinary." If you break it down, what does this mean? Nothing more than "beyond the ordinary." But this is exactly what passion fuels: it takes us from a banal, uninspired everyday existence and pushes us to soar to greater and greater heights.

And ultimately, it leads us to a place where we can be content. Not content with what we've done to date, which implies reaching a static equilibrium, but rather in the fact that we know, in our heart, that we are going places and doing things. That we are not standing still, but instead constantly pushing our own limits. This is invigorating. This is exciting. This is emancipating. By making passion your lodestar, you become truly free.

You are living the dream. Not every minute of every hour of every day, of course. But your trajectory will take you further than you ever thought you'd be able to go. And from this process—self-knowledge, confidence, forging an intimate connection with what you want and who you are at your core—flows a holistic sense of purpose.

To use a chef's metaphor: passion is the mother sauce. So much can be built upon it. Find it. Use it. Go forward and do great things.

VINCENT VAN GOGH:
FAILURE TO LAUNCH

IT IS A SPECTACULAR HOMAGE. The touring exhibition *Imagine Van Gogh*, a collection of massively recreated paintings, actually leaves very little to the imagination. From Vincent van Gogh's time in Arles to his final days in Auvers-sur-Oise, the multimedia extravaganza shows the incredible breadth and undeniable passion of a man who, although today revered as one of the finest artists ever, probably managed to sell just one canvas while he was alive.

Born in 1853 to an upper-middle-class Dutch family, Van Gogh was a classic late bloomer. After trying his hand at evangelism, teaching, and art brokering, he finally began painting in earnest at the age of 27. His early career was not particularly promising, but he soon began to experiment with different styles and techniques. An admirer of the Dutch masters such as Vermeer and Rembrandt, he adopted some of their trademark stylistic tics: the use of muted colors and respect for the impact of light and shadow.

In 1886, broke and desperate, Van Gogh relocated to Paris and moved in with his brother, Theo. It was auspicious timing. At the time, Paris was practically teeming with artists whose names would become synonymous with the Impressionism and Post-Impressionism movements. Among those whom Van Gogh admired were Claude Monet, who had practically come to define the Impressionist style, and Georges Seurat, whose "pointillist" paintings were composed of thousands of tiny dots—another revolutionary approach. The canvases of Adolphe Monticelli, who used densely applied paint in his still-life paintings, would also be a major influence. Van Gogh absorbed what he could and tried his hand at many different techniques.

Paris was his training ground, the jumping-off point for what Van Gogh would become. Although he was an admirer of his contemporaries, he was also creating a style that was uniquely his. He applied paint in thick gobs, using dots, squiggles, and radiating lines to create a vibrancy to his art. It was as if the paintings themselves held an energy that was constantly being released. An early colour palette that was by turns sombre and dark—as seen in *The Potato Eaters*, a moody portrait of a peasant family at dinner—began to change, becoming wildly bright and vivid: pulsating yellows and reds, along with the churning hues of his self-portraits, which hinted at the psychological disruption that would at one point consume him. Lamps flared with a fiery intensity, and skies glowed surreally—a swirling, chaotic cosmos.

It was like nothing else. It was both primitive and refined. It was, by and large, ignored. The sole exception: *The Red Vineyard in Arles*, the only work we know for certain that the artist sold during his lifetime. It brought him 400 francs.

Still, Van Gogh soldiered on, continuing to paint at an almost feverish pace. His art consumed him and gave him purpose. Yet Paris, while an incubator of talent, was not where he would find his muse. In 1888, Van Gogh moved to the south of France. His technical skill continued to blossom, and many of his most famous works—*Sunflowers, The Night Cafe, A Starry Night*—were painted after he settled in Provence. There, he dreamed of creating an artist's colony where inspiration, ideas, and camaraderie could be shared.

To that end, he rented a home in Arles and invited the painter Paul Gauguin to move in. But the relationship was volatile, and the two fought bitterly during the nine-week cohabitation experiment. On December 23, 1888, in a state of emotional distress after a fight with Gauguin, Van Gogh cut off his ear— the whole ear aside from the lobe—and gave it to a cleaner at a local brothel. Gauguin left, and while the two continued to correspond, they never saw each other again.

Towards the end of his life, Van Gogh's mental health, always fragile, began to unwind. Anxiety and depression had dogged him for years, but he began to suffer from full-scale psychotic episodes. In 1889, he checked himself into an asylum, where he stayed for almost a year. It was a prelude to his final act. On July 27, 1890, Van Gogh shot himself in the chest with a revolver. Thirty hours later, he died.

In his short, nine-year career as a working artist, Van Gogh produced over 900 paintings, a prodigious output. While most of his most famous pieces are housed in public museums, a few works continue to be sold privately. The most expensive: the brooding *Portrait of Dr. Gachet*, which sold for nearly US$83 million in 1990, a century after Van Gogh painted it. As testament to his enduring and expanding popularity, today it would probably fetch almost double.

A LIFE WITHOUT PASSION?

"We're going through!" The Commander's voice was like thin ice breaking. He wore his full-dress uniform, with the heavily braided white cap pulled down rakishly over one cold gray eye. "We can't make it, sir. It's spoiling for a hurricane, if you ask me." "I'm not asking you, Lieutenant Berg," said the Commander. "Throw on the power lights! Rev her up to 8,500! We're going through!" The pounding of the cylinders increased: ta-pocketa-pocketa-pocketa-pocketa-pocketa. The Commander stared at the ice forming on the pilot window. He walked over and twisted a row of complicated dials...

FROM "THE SECRET LIFE OF WALTER MITTY"

FOR A COMEDIC PIECE, James Thurber's 1939 short story "The Secret Life of Walter Mitty" is one of the saddest tales I have ever read. In it, the protagonist, a henpecked, mild-mannered man, is dropping his wife off at the hairdresser. While waiting for her and mechanically carrying out the boring tasks she has assigned, he whiles away the time by daydreaming. Full of danger and adventure, the daydreams are the opposite of Mitty's feeble, milquetoast existence. In them he is the commander of a Navy hydroplane, navigating the threatening waters of an angry sea. He is a famous surgeon, called in to save the life of a millionaire banker (who is also a close friend of U.S. President Franklin Delano Roosevelt, of course). He is a sharpshooter accused of murder, a fighter pilot who can "hold his brandy." Finally, condemned to die, he takes a final drag of his cigarette and faces a firing squad with boundless reserves of stoic courage: "To hell with the handkerchief." He meets his death bravely, unchanged and unapologetic, and, as Thurber sums up, "inscrutable to the last."

A lot of people love this story. The moral, some have decided, is that Mitty accepts himself for who he is: *inscrutable to the last*. I have a much different takeaway. Walter Mitty has spent his entire life wishing, wanting. That he would do great things or be a great person. That he would—that he *could*—be someone who he is not.

Mitty is a case study in denial, a man who has submerged his own passion so deeply that it exists only in his imagination. He has lived his entire adult life as an errand boy for a domineering and dismissive partner. His accomplishments? Nothing. His self-worth? Zero. His only pleasure is found by creating exciting and fanciful futures that he hasn't the courage to pursue.

Walter Mitty is the poster child for who you do not want to be.

———

To truly know what a life lived passionately can bring, we need to look at its opposite. So, what would a life without passion look like? We don't need the help of fiction to visualize this. You see it every day.

The guy who punches a clock and shuffles back to his house to slump on the sofa to eat dinner from a can while watching TV, a bottle of Pabst Blue Ribbon fixed in his hand. The investment banker who, after raking in another multimillion-dollar bonus cheque, decides that nothing she has ever done has created anything of true or lasting value, and slides into the driver's seat of her Bentley with the engine running and the garage door closed. The government worker who chooses "pension over passion" and drags himself to his workplace every day until he retires on his 60th birthday—and a few days later hears his doctor say, in the gentlest way possible, that there's a lump in his neck and he should put his affairs in order.

All of these examples are unbearably sad, mainly because they are unbelievably common. These are people who have no end game to aim for, and so their goals are scattershot and often without purpose. *I want to make more money. I want to be skinny. I want to look young. I want to eat healthily so I can live a long life.* To what end? On their own, none of these goals propels you toward anything of consequence or value. This is because they are superfluous. Because they are not moved forward by our core passions, these goals are devoid of real meaning. They are markers, but only just. Barometers of somebody else's idea of accomplishment.

Finding your passion doesn't mean pursuing one singular path. Instead, it becomes a *way of life*, one that ports over into other areas and enriches in a variety of situations. It leads to the discovery of new opportunities and nurtures growth and advancement. Even in my 80s, I'm still vividly excited about new goals and the dreams and opportunities that await. I treat every day as an opportunity to discover something new about myself and the direction I've taken.

As I get older, my goals have shifted—but the underlying passion, the desire to challenge myself and overcome hurdles, remains the same. For example, releasing a book a year and podcasting twice a week are two newer challenges that excite me. But neither would have been possible if I hadn't pursued other dreams earlier in life. Like, for example, moving to Canada—the land of my heroes—and starting my own lumber mill. These are dreams that cascaded and spawned other dreams. But the motivating heart of it all was passion.

I can confidently say that in order to live life to the fullest, you need to understand that at some point it will end. The best advice I've ever heard was a quote from Gandhi: "Live each day as if you will die tomorrow. Learn as if you will live forever."

But always, and above all, live with passion.

This has been quite the journey! I hope you agree.

Passion, as we've discovered, is a multifaceted and very nuanced concept. It can manifest as rebellion—depending on who happens to be leading it, for good or ill. It can be subversive, again for the same reasons. It can send humankind to the farthest reaches of our solar system and to the bottom of the deepest ocean. It gave us democracy, science, philosophy, computers, and every major work of art ever created.

Behind all the great gifts that humanity has bestowed upon itself, an abiding passion has been the prime motivating force.

For those who seek it, passion is a voyage of self-discovery, a journey to the very heart of who you truly are and who you want to be. By locking into your passion, you also lock into who you are on almost a subatomic level—what makes you tick, what makes you happy, what fulfills your desire. At times, pursuing that desire will test you: life is a marathon, not a 100-yard dash. For those who face difficult challenges—and that would be most of us at some point—there will be times when you question the path you're on. But that's what grit and perseverance are all about.

Armed with passion, you will do great things. You will feel that your life has meaning. You will view challenges not only as things to be overcome but as points of departure, new paths toward other goals. With passion, a positive attitude, and a committed work ethic as your animating principles, there is nothing that can stop you.

And so, we come to the final page. I want to commend you for undertaking this journey and wish you good fortune on your quest to let your truest desire be the light that guides you and propels you forward—against any and all odds.

With my sincerest thanks for our time together, I remain

Passionately yours,

JOHN A. BRINK

John A. Brink is President and CEO of Brink Forest Products, one of the largest forestry companies in British Columbia. He is the founding President of the B.C. Council of Value-Added Wood Processors. In addition to his success in business, John is a dedicated philanthropist and long-time supporter of amateur and professional athletes. He is a nationally ranked competitive bodybuilder and rides dressage weekly with his wife, Sharon. John is a member of the Order of British Columbia and a Distinguished Toastmaster. He holds an honorary Doctor of Laws degree from the University of Northern British Columbia. He lives in Prince George and North Saanich, British Columbia. John has lived his entire life with attention-deficit/hyperactivity disorder (ADHD).